PENGUIN

17

SIX GREAT A

LORD BIRKETT

LORD BIRKETT

SIX GREAT ADVOCATES

PENGUIN BOOKS

Penguin Books Ltd, Harmondsworth, Middlesex
U.S.A.: Penguin Books Inc., 3300 Clipper Mill Road, Baltimore 11, Md
AUSTRALIA: Penguin Books Pty Ltd, 762 Whitehorse Road,
Mitcham, Victoria

—

First published 1961
Reprinted 1963

—

Copyright © Lord Birkett, 1961

—

Made and printed in Great Britain
by C. Nicholls & Company Ltd
Set in Monotype Times

CONTENTS

PREFACE

I SHOULD perhaps explain briefly how this book comes into being. I was invited by the British Broadcasting Corporation to contribute to the Home Service Programme a series of talks on six great advocates, and to wind up the series with a general talk on advocacy. I was glad to do this and the talks were broadcast on seven Sunday evenings in April and May 1961. They were thirty-minute talks and were written and delivered in the hope that they might provide entertainment and pleasure by recalling some of the great figures at the English Bar and some of the cases by which they are best remembered. I felt a particular pleasure in writing and speaking of those advocates I had known and admired, and an almost equal pleasure in speaking of those advocates whose fame, almost legendary with lawyers, is handed on from generation to generation.

The broadcast talks were generously received by listeners, and I was gratified to find that they interested many who were not connected with the law in any way. Many listeners wrote to me and to the BBC to ask whether the talks could be published. I was at first reluctant to do this for I have always felt the truth of Hazlitt's famous essay 'On the Difference Between Speaking and Writing', and indeed made reference to the substance of the essay when speaking of the magnetic eloquence of Marshall Hall. But when Penguin Books Ltd very kindly suggested the publication of the talks, I felt that this was the appropriate form for a collection of talks of this kind and I am most grateful for the suggestion.

My recent experience has made me think with some

pleasure that the fame of the advocate is not quite so fleeting and transient as is sometimes supposed; and my reflections on the art of advocacy in the concluding chapter have shown me from their reception how deep is the interest of the general public in all matters appertaining to the administration of the law and in the advocates who take part in it.

I would like to add that these talks were produced in the Home Service by Mr Joe Burroughs and they owe much to his knowledge and experience of broadcasting, and to his feeling for what Swift called 'proper words in proper places'. I am glad to record my indebtedness to him.

BIRKETT

SIR EDWARD MARSHALL HALL, K.C.

MARSHALL HALL was universally and affectionately known to the public as well as to the law. I knew him well and was in his chambers for the last seven years of his life. He was then still at the height of his powers, and I saw him in all his many moods, from exultation to despair.

In the thirty years since his death he has become almost a legendary figure in the public mind, owing, in some degree, to the work of his brilliant biographer, Edward Marjoribanks. He likened Marshall Hall to the great forensic orator of Rome, Hortensius, whose fame survives after two thousand years because of his splendid physical presence, the adulation of the public, and his powers of eloquent and persuasive speech. We shall not look upon Marshall's like again, for the age that produced him, and gloried in his spectacular triumphs in the courts, has passed away for ever. The advocate no longer plays the part in our public life that he once did. The fashionable divorce suit, the sensational libel action, the great murder trial – they are no longer the dramatic events that once occupied public attention to the exclusion of almost everything else. The television star and the film actor or actress, idolized by millions, now take pride of place. But men must be judged by the standards of the age in which they lived and worked, and, in his day, Marshall Hall was one of the great figures of his world. He was one of the greatest of advocates when he was at his best.

I make this important qualification because it is necessary to make it. It is not enough to say that Marshall Hall was an erratic genius; he was certainly that; but there were times and occasions when genius was simply not there. He had almost all the qualities that go to make the great advocate. He had sympathy and understanding; he could enter fully into the lives of other people almost naturally; he had fire and passion and zeal; he was dramatic and histrionic; he could speak simply and most attractively to ordinary people; and, as his outstanding quality, he could rise to heights of pure eloquence and sway the hearts and minds of men. But he had grievous shortcomings that might so easily have destroyed a lesser man. He was the strangest mixture of perfections and imperfections that I ever knew at the Bar. Sometimes with his quick mind and almost uncanny perception of the important point in the case, he would seize it, throw away every carefully conceived plan, and win the victory against all odds; and then, at other times, when he was at the most important stage of some other case, he would be suddenly and unaccountably blind to the most obvious considerations. His judgment would seem to desert him, and he himself would become quite bewildered and lost. In the Russell divorce suit in 1923, Sir Douglas Hogg, the Attorney General, was asked to suggest the name of counsel to conduct the case. Sir Douglas and Sir John Simon had both failed in the previous trial, and were not now available for the rehearing. Sir Douglas said, 'There's only one man at the Bar who might pull it off for you. He might win you a brilliant victory or he might make a terrible mess of it; but I believe that he's the only man who *can* do it – get Marshall Hall.' And Marshall did pull it off in the most brilliant fashion. But this saying of Sir Douglas Hogg is the wise and experienced comment of a great friend, and expresses very clearly the strange mixture of which the genius of Marshall Hall was compounded.

Marshall Hall was born at Brighton in 1858. His father was a well-known physician, from whom Marshall learnt a great deal about medicine, and in particular about poisons. Marshall used this knowledge with immense effect in many of his cases, most notably when he defended Frederick Seddon in 1912. His cross-examination of the Home-Office expert, Sir William Willcox, is still regarded as a model of what such a cross-examination should be, both because of the scientific knowledge of arsenical poisoning Marshall displayed, and for the psychological skill with which he almost brought Sir William to admit the vital point for which he was contending. I have always thought it was typical of Marshall Hall that at the age of fourteen he decided to go to the Bar just because of one morning he spent in the Magistrates' Court at Brighton. A woman named Christiana Edmunds was charged with murder by the administration of the poison known as strychnine. She had bought quantities of strychnine and inserted some of it into chocolates; but the manner in which counsel told the story to the magistrates so captivated the youthful Marshall that he was at once irrevocably resolved to be an advocate himself. That idea was later replaced by a burning ambition to be a clergyman and a popular preacher, and this idea was in turn abandoned: and then after a good deal of indecision Marshall was finally called to the Bar by the Inner Temple in 1883.

I first saw Marshall Hall, as defending counsel in a trial for murder, when he was briefed for a young schoolmaster at the Leicester Assizes in 1920, in what became known as the Green Bicycle Case. I was briefed as junior counsel for the Crown, with Gordon Hewart and Henry Maddocks leading me. It was the first murder case of note in which I was briefed, and naturally I remember almost every detail of the trial. I shall always remember the moment when Marshall Hall came into court at Leicester Castle. He brought with him a strange magnetic quality that made itself felt in every part of the court. The spectators stirred with excitement at the sight of the man whose name was at that time a household word, and a faint murmur ran from floor to gallery. Marshall came, of course, with all the prestige of the greatest criminal defender of the day, and every eye was fixed upon him. He was a very handsome man, with noble head and a most expressive face, and F. E. Smith's comment is not to be bettered: 'Nobody could have been as wonderful as Marshall Hall then looked.' When he addressed the judge it was seen that to his great good looks and majestic bearing there had been added perhaps the greatest gift of all in the armoury of an advocate—a most beautiful speaking voice. He had in this case a terrible task before him.

A young girl, Bella Wright, had been found dead on a country road near the Leicestershire village of Gaulby. She had been shot through the head and a bullet was found close to the body. On the night before her body was found she was seen in the company of a young man at the house of her uncle. The young man called her Bella and was obviously very friendly; and he had a green bicycle. For seven long months the death of Bella Wright was a complete mystery, but one day a canal boatman, taking a load to a factory, saw his towrope slacken and then tauten, and bring to the surface a green bicycle; and a revolver holster and cartridges were later recovered from the same spot. The green bicycle was identified as having been sold to the young schoolmaster. When he was seen by the police, he said he did not know anybody called Bella Wright, he had not been in her company, he had

12

never been near the village of Gaulby on the night in question, and he had never had a green bicycle. Later he said that he *had* had a green bicycle but had sold it years ago. At the magistrates' court the defending counsel had suggested by his questions that the defence of the young schoolmaster would be an alibi. When Sir Gordon Hewart, the Attorney General, concluded this narrative to the jury it seemed to me at the time to be quite unanswerable. But Marshall Hall was always at his best when things looked blackest. He had seen the only possible line of defence and he discarded everything else. He frankly admitted that the young schoolmaster *was* with Bella Wright that night; that the green bicycle *was* his; that he had thrown it into the canal after storing it in his rooms for many months; that the revolver holster and cartridges *were* his; that he had lied continuously to the police but had acted out of sheer panic and fear. The one line Marshall left open was that the young schoolmaster was never on the road that night where the dead body of Bella Wright was found next morning. And the speech of Marshall Hall to the jury was the most astonishing piece of advocacy I had ever heard up to that time. Knowing the details of the case as I did, I listened to his every word with a fascinated wonder and amazement. When he came to his peroration and depicted the figure of Justice holding the scales until the presumption of innocence was put there to turn the scale in favour of the prisoner, not only were the jury manifestly impressed, but they, and indeed the whole court, were under a kind of spell.

The intensity and passion of Marshall Hall in moments like these had to be seen to be believed. It was simply overpowering and juries were swept off their feet. After that memorable day I saw him in almost every kind of case, but he excelled in those cases where the human interest was strong. He had the rare gift of using true pathos in his advocacy, and such a device in the hands of men less obviously sincere would have sounded artificial and wrong. He was the only advocate I ever saw who wept before the jury and allowed the tears to stream down his cheeks as he spoke. It was the greatest of gifts for it seemed so natural that nobody felt it to be in any sense theatrical: it seemed to be just an essential part of his passionately sincere pleading. Certainly, Marshall's tears never provoked Tim Healy's acid comment on the theatrical tears of an insincere opponent: 'Gentlemen of the jury, you have just witnessed the greatest miracle since Moses struck the rock in the wilderness.'

Marshall Hall's claim to remembrance as an advocate is based almost wholly on his triumphs as a defender in trials for murder. It was in fact a murder case that first made his name widely known and set him on the road to fame. And since that first murder case so well illustrates the quality of swift unthinking action that sometimes marked his advocacy, it is most interesting as being the first time he displayed it and with marked success. He had waited eleven years for an opportunity such as this and now it was here; and he took it with a characteristic flourish.

The facts were painfully sordid, as they so often are. A poor destitute woman of forty-three, known to the police as a harlot, was charged at the Central Criminal Court with murder, and Marshall was given the brief for the defence because there was no money to brief any better-known man. The woman's name was Marie Hermann, an Austrian, who had been a governess and a teacher of music and had known better days. She had taken to her sordid way of life to earn a living for herself and her children. She was a small, emaciated woman who had had a terrible life of suffering and tragedy. The evidence was: that one night there had been loud noises coming from Marie Hermann's room and a man's voice calling 'Murder' thrice repeated. The next day Marie Hermann announced that she was leaving, and amongst her belongings was a large trunk which was later found to contain the body of a man who had died from being struck many times with an iron bar. The defence was that she had picked up this man who was drunk, that he had no money, and that because she would not submit to him in those circumstances he had seized her by the throat and had taken hold of the iron bar. She got the iron bar from him and hit him several times, but had later gone out for brandy and bandages, and had tried to restore him; but the man had died.

Marshall Hall fought for this poor woman for three days. He did two things that were to be repeated in many of his subsequent cases. First, he made a dramatic reconstruction of the crime before the jury, and acted the part of Marie Hermann with the iron bar, showing that what he suggested had actually taken place. This, it will be recalled, was the very thing he did with such startling effect thirty years later, when he defended Madame Fahmy at the Old Bailey on the charge of shooting her husband. During his closing speech at that trial, he actually crouched before the jury with the pistol in his hand, imitating the oriental crouch of the husband approaching his wife with intent to injure her, and Madame Fahmy's raising of the pistol as he came in; and in when, his reconstruction to the jury, he reached the moment when the pistol went off and the husband fell, Marshall let the pistol fall to the floor of the court with a tremendous clatter, just as it must have fallen on the corridor of the

Savoy Hotel on the night of the tragedy. Whether Marshall had foreseen this moment I am not sure. He always said that he let the pistol fall accidentally; but the sudden breaking of the intense stillness of the court by the noise of the falling pistol produced the most extraordinary effect on everybody present, almost as though they had witnessed the actual tragedy itself.

The second thing Marshall Hall did in the Marie Hermann case illustrates that quality of his advocacy which I always thought was the source of some of his greatest successes; but at the same time was at the root of some of his failures. It was his sometimes irresistible impulse to act on the spur of the moment. In his final speech to the jury in the Marie Hermann case he said, 'Gentlemen of the Jury, I beg you to cast aside all prejudice because of this woman's way of life. I beg you to remember that these women are what men make them; even this woman was once a beautiful and innocent child.' At these words Marie Hermann broke down and wept uncontrollably, remembering no doubt those happier days. In this tense moment Marshall Hall said slowly, and almost defiantly, 'Gentlemen, on this evidence I almost dare you to find a verdict of guilty.' He turned to sit down, but as he did so he suddenly caught sight of this weeping woman, bent with grief in the dock, the very picture of human misery and desolation; and it touched the depths of his warm heart. In a flash he straightened himself and turned to the jury once more, and in a voice no longer defiant, but trembling with pity and compassion he said in tones of sheer entreaty as he pointed to her broken figure in the dock: 'Look at her, Gentlemen of the Jury, look at her. God never gave her a chance. Won't you? Won't you?' There is no other counsel I ever saw who could have done it. It was so obviously spontaneous and sincere; as

though he had said: 'For God's sake have pity on her!'
We are told that the effect in the court was profound.
Charles Mathews who prosecuted, and was himself one
of the last great forensic orators, was deeply moved;
but without the background of that harrowing scene
where Marshall was throwing his protecting arms around
this sobbing woman to shield her, without that face of
tears and that pleading voice, instinct with compassion, it
is quite impossible at this distance of time really to
appreciate the effect. To those who saw and heard it
there can be no doubt of its profundity. Many of Marshall
Hall's speeches can be read today in the law reports and
elsewhere, but they give no clue whatever to the emotions
of the moment when they were delivered. Sometimes
they sound mawkish and sentimental, sometimes even
tawdry to our way of thinking. But we should remember
that we read them without the fire and glow of Marshall's
physical presence. The dramatic setting of the court has
vanished, and the thing said has been separated from the
moment of its saying; and all those 'brave sublunary
things', as Hazlitt called them, that made the moment
memorable are irrevocably gone. Nothing could be plainer
than the fact that great advocacy is designed for some
particular occasion. The advocate himself with his own
distinctive presence and personality, his quick resilient
mind, his resource, his sense of the occasion; his particular
theme, whether lofty and noble, or tragic and pitiful; the
form and beauty of his speech designed for the occasion,
its fire and glow and vehemence, his gestures, the tone of
his voice, the expression of his face – all these things are
for one particular occasion, and once the occasion has
gone, all these things are gone too and can never be
recalled, except perhaps by the exercise of sympathetic
imagination. And even that is only a substitute, and not

always a fair and just substitute, for the occasion itself.

When Marshall Hall defended Marie Hermann in 1894 he had passed through a domestic tragedy of his own of the most grievous kind. His first marriage, through no fault of his own, was a complete disaster, and ended in the most dreadful tragedy that anybody could conceive. He carried the scars of that tragedy to the end of his life and he wrote in his diary at the time, 'Words can never tell my grief.' I have never doubted that his own personal sorrows had made him wonderfully sympathetic to the sorrows of others, and with his emotional and susceptible temperament he was easily led to extremes which sometimes led him to the heights, but on occasion brought him to the depths.

In the year that I went into his chambers in London – it was in 1920 – he defended a solicitor named Harold Greenwood on the charge of murder by administering arsenic to his wife by putting it into the wine she drank at dinner. The trial took place at Carmarthen Assizes and public opinion was for various reasons intensely hostile to the prisoner. Marshall Hall transformed public opinion by his masterly conduct of the case, as he had done in the case of Robert Wood in 1907, and in the Green Bicycle case thirteen years later. Here again he ended on a dramatic note, but on this occasion a quite unusual note for him, for it was most carefully prepared and rehearsed. It was not so effective perhaps as his impetuous action in the case of Marie Hermann, but it emphasized the point every defending counsel must make in every case, in one form or another: the duty of the prosecution to prove the case against the prisoner beyond all reasonable doubt. Marshall's closing words were directed to this vital point and this is what he said, echoing his defence of Seddon eight years before:

'Gentlemen of the Jury, the case for the Prosecution has now been utterly exploded. It was begun by local gossip; it depended for its details on the prompted and uncertain memory of a servant girl, and for its scientific justification on the finding in the body of the bare minimum quantity of arsenic necessary for a fatal dose, by means of an elaborate and fallible experiment. Gentlemen of the Jury, your verdict is final. Science can do a great deal. These men with their mirrors, multipliers, and milligrammes can tell you to the thousandth or millionth part of a grain the constituents of the human body. But there is one thing science can never do. It cannot find the vital spark which converts insensate clay into a human being.'

Here Marshall dropped his voice to a whisper and quoted the famous words used by Othello when he stole into Desdemona's chamber:

> 'Put out the light, and then put out the light:
> If I quench thee, thou flaming minister,
> I can again thy former light restore,
> Should I repent me. But once put out thy light,
> Thou cunning'st pattern of excelling Nature,
> I know not where is that Promethean heat
> That can thy light re-lume.'

Then in the same low voice he said to the jury: 'Are you going by your verdict to put out that light?' And then in clear ringing tones, he said: 'No; Gentlemen of the Jury, I demand at your hands the life and liberty of Harold Greenwood.' The verdict was not guilty.

Many criticisms of Marshall Hall may be heard, and two of them I will just mention. It was said of him that his knowledge of law was scanty and that he was too ready to quarrel with judges. Both charges are true. They probably explain in part why Marshall was never made a judge; and he himself withdrew his application to be made the Recorder of London in circumstances which do him the highest credit. Marshall was the first to acknowledge his ignorance of law, but knowledge of the law was never an indispensable qualification for the advocate. For his purposes, Marshall's knowledge of human nature was the very richest possession, and far outweighed any shortcomings in the deeper mysteries of the law. His inability to control his temper and his tongue when irritated by some behaviour of the judge was undoubtedly a grave defect; and dearly he paid for it. But some of the judges with whom he quarrelled were equally to blame for their inconsiderate behaviour and hasty words, and one of them at least was thought at the time to be animated by malice. These things are blemishes no doubt, but of those who say that Marshall Hall was not a great advocate I ask: who can match his record of triumphant advocacy and the wonderful verdicts which he won from the juries? With all his faults of temper or temperament he was always himself, and he never attempted to imitate or copy anybody else. In a very famous trial during the First World War, when a young British lieutenant was charged with killing a man who had tried to take his wife away from him when he was on active service, Marshall had a watching brief only, and Sir John Simon conducted the defence. Marshall always said that Simon's closing speech was the finest piece of advocacy he ever heard; but he never tried to imitate it. The truth was that it was eloquence of quite another order from his, and Marshall knew it.

There are no fixed and unalterable standards of advocacy. It is impossible to point to a John Simon or a Marshall Hall and to say: There is the pattern. Lord

Rosebery once catalogued some of the qualities which made Lord Chatham the greatest orator of his age, and when he had set them all out – the right choice of words, the elegance of the sentences, the poetical imagination, the passion, the mordant wit, the great dramatic skill – he added these impressive words: 'A clever fellow who had mastered all these things would produce but a pale reflection of the original. It is not merely the thing that is said but the man who says it that counts, the character which breathes through the sentences.' So it was with Marshall at his best. He could never be imitated. He was the last of his kind and none of his successors has ever taken his place. For the status of the advocate has changed and the style of advocacy has changed too. But whenever advocacy is being discussed, the name and fame of Marshall Hall will occupy a foremost place as one of the greatest exponents of the art; and that name and fame the world will not willingly let die.

Sir Patrick Hastings, K.C.

It is now more than twelve years since the voice of Patrick Hastings was heard in the courts of law but there are many people who retain very vivid recollections of that remarkable man. Others have spoken of his brief career in the House of Commons when he became the Attorney General in the first Labour Government, and of his work as a playwright; but I am quite sure that his claim to public remembrance must rest upon his achievements as one of the outstandingly brilliant advocates of his day and generation.

I suppose I knew him better than most people outside his own family circle, because there was a time in the thirties when we were almost daily opponents, practising before juries in the civil courts. I admired him from the very moment I first saw him, as I shall tell; but in later years affection was added to admiration. This was a little remarkable, because we differed so greatly in background and outlook, and most of all in personal tastes. Looking back over the years, I think we both took a considerable risk in deciding to go to the Bar. There was a belief in some quarters, which still exists in some measure, that without a private income success at the Bar is very uncertain; and neither of us had any reserves to tide us over the early days of waiting for briefs to come. I suppose that because we had both survived the hazards of a highly competitive profession we were drawn to each other a little more closely; but whatever it was there was certainly some kind of bond between us. It is strange that this should be so, for although Patrick Hastings disliked some people and said so, sometimes with great rudeness, and even found it difficult on occasion to be polite to an opponent, I do not recall that we ever had what could properly be called a quarrel. The truth is that Patrick Hastings was quite unlike any other advocate of his time. Sometimes perhaps he sought to emulate the methods of Charles Russell and Edward Carson, those two powerful, dominating personalities he so much admired, but for the most part he was content to let his own personality have full play. Nobody would ever dream of calling Hastings eccentric, but in certain matters appertaining to advocacy he was quite outside the accepted tradition.

The strongest weapon in the armoury of the advocate is usually said to be the gift of speech. In rare and exceptional cases it can be the gift of true eloquence, so persuasive that, as Ben Jonson said of the speaking of Francis Bacon, 'His hearers could not cough or look aside from him without loss. . . . The fear of every man that heard him was lest he should make an end.' But Hastings affected to disdain the arts of speech. He could be very contemptuous of passionate appeals made to juries by advocates like Marshall Hall. 'Bombast' and 'humbug' were the words he would apply in private and, if necessity warranted, in public too. My own belief is that the command of English enriches and adorns almost every other quality of the advocate, but is very far from being all. Patrick Hastings was by no means a great speaker in the conventional sense. He was certainly not in the tradition of Sheridan, Charles James Fox, Edmund Burke, or the younger Pitt. He was not a great reader, and his mind was not stored with the riches of English literature or the great speeches of orators in ancient and modern times. It was quite characteristic of him that he should affect to be scornful of forensic oratory of the flamboyant kind because it was quite alien to his style of advocacy, and really outside his range; for in all that he did he seemed to want to put himself in a category of his own.

He had succeeded at the Bar against great odds. Born in 1880, the son of a solicitor, he had a curious childhood, alternating between poverty and affluence. In one of his father's more prosperous periods he spent two years at Charterhouse, but always said that he learnt nothing that was of any practical value to him. When he was at last called to the Bar by the Middle Temple he was quite penniless, and these early struggles had made him self-reliant and independent and very much inclined to go his own way wherever that might lead him. It is interesting to recall that on that night in 1904 when the Benchers of the Middle Temple called him to the Bar, he was wearing a wig and gown which he had obtained on credit, and when he had paid the necessary fee of £100 which he had slowly gathered together, he had nothing left but his own wits. But they were to prove more than enough to bring him to the top of his profession and to great rewards. When I first saw Patrick Hastings the days of poverty were gone and his feet were already firmly planted on the road to fame. His biographer, Mr Montgomery Hyde, states that for many years Hastings earned £40,000 a year, and when I first knew him it was the magnificence of his motor cars and his supremely confident manner that I remember as being expressive of the desire to be different from other men.

He well knew his limitations, and he knew where his strength lay. He knew that the modes of speech in advocacy are of various kinds, and each one of them can be effective in the hands of the right man. Hastings had a very powerful kind of his own. He was a master of simple, direct, forcible speech without any embellishments or ornamentation. He also knew the immense value of concise speech linked with brevity; and some of his speeches, without any attempt at literary grace or adornment, were as effective as anything I ever heard from more dramatic or picturesque orators. Hastings' reputation does not rest on spectacular defences in murder trials – he did only one of note and that he did superbly – indeed he avoided murder cases if he could. His practice was almost wholly in the civil courts and very largely before juries. Divorce, libel, fraud – these were the fields where Hastings shone. Today the jury has practically disappeared from civil cases and the style of advocacy has been profoundly affected in consequence. To attempt eloquence before a judge alone is slightly ridiculous, and it was said of one great jury advocate that he always refused non-jury cases lest they should spoil his style.

But the great quality of Hastings as an advocate was his power of cross-examination. He was without doubt the greatest cross-examiner I ever heard or saw. When I first set eyes on him – and that was almost by chance – he was doing that very thing: conducting a tremendous cross-examination in a crowded court, not only with immense power and effect, but with a concentrated ruthlessness that was really terrible to behold. I can never forget the emotions of the moment when I entered that court and saw for the first time the spare, straight figure of Hastings, as junior counsel in the back row, contending with two leading counsel of considerable fame – Rigby Swift and Douglas Hogg. It is a faraway moment now, but it is the moment I most often recall when I think of Patrick, because it was undoubtedly his finest hour.

He was cross-examining a prominent Liberal Member of Parliament called Handel Booth, who was, as I well knew, the Member for Pontefract, and very active he was in the House of Commons. A German named Gruban, a very clever engineer, who had been in this country for several years, had built up a very fine business in Oldham when war broke out in 1914. He became naturalized but required some additional capital and had been advised to seek the help of Handel Booth. Booth had taken a leading part in what was known as the Marconi case, in which Mr Lloyd George was concerned, and Mr Lloyd George was supposed to be indebted to Booth for what he had done; at least Booth said so. Lloyd George was then Minister of Munitions. When the *Lusitania* was sunk by the Germans there was a great wave of anti-German feeling in this country, and Gruban was anxious lest his contracts with the Government for machine tools would be cancelled. He confided his fears to Booth who said, 'If you can get me on your company, I can do what I like with the Ministry of Munitions.' The result was that Booth was made Chairman of the company. He began to draw hundreds of pounds from the firm but was greedy for more. He wanted a secret commission of ten per cent on a certain £6,000 contract. Gruban refused because he thought it was dishonest. Booth had already written a little note setting out that he should have £600, and when Gruban refused Booth crumpled up the paper in anger and threw it into the waste paper basket. From then onwards, behind Gruban's back, Booth did everything he could to injure Gruban. He told him he would probably be interned, and the only way to remain free was to hand over his shareholding to Booth, to take no further part in the management, and to let Booth act as his Trustee. Gruban felt compelled to agree but notwithstanding all this he was in fact interned. He appealed to a Tribunal and his case, fortunately for him, was heard by two

English judges who ordered his instant release and went out of their way to tell Gruban that he should see a solicitor to get proper protection for his interests. The solicitor issued a writ and briefed Hastings to conduct the case for Gruban against Booth. The claim was for damages for fraud and it was heard by Lord Coleridge and a jury.

Now, nobody was better than Hastings in conducting a case where fraud was charged. To hear him pronounce the words 'swindler' and 'rogue' could be quite startling for the venom he put into the words; and when he opened the case to the jury, his speech was scathing and lacerating. Gruban and his wife were the only witnesses for the plaintiff, and after Rigby Swift had opened the case for the defence he called Handel Booth into the witness box. Booth denied every allegation of fraud, and most indignantly denied that he had ever sought a ten-per-cent commission for himself. But before the cross-examination of Booth began, the evidence of Dr Addison, who had succeeded Lloyd George as Minister of Munitions, was interposed, and in two questions to him, Hastings, with that gift of lucidity and brevity of which I have spoken, put the whole case against Booth.

'Dr Addison,' said Hastings, 'had you at any time been advising Mr Handel Booth as to what course Mr Gruban should adopt?' and the answer was, 'Certainly not.'

'Dr Addison,' said Hastings, 'if Mr Booth had ever stated that you had told him that Gruban's only chance of escaping internment was that he should hand over all his shares to Mr Handel Booth, would that statement have been a lie?' And the answer was 'It would.'

Hastings once confided to me that he usually thought out his first question in cross-examination with great care, and he fastened on Booth's denial of ever demanding a secret commission at once, and this is how the cross-examination opened:

'Mr Handel Booth, would it be dishonest for a director of a company to seek for himself a secret commission on his company's earnings?'

To which Booth with great emphasis said, 'Of course it would.'

'If you did such a thing, would you consider yourself a rogue?'

To which Booth answered even more emphatically: 'Of course.'

'Did you do that very thing when you were a Director of Gruban's company?'

To which Booth, almost speechless with indignation, shouted: 'Never, never, never!'

'Very well,' said Hastings quietly, 'take a look at this piece of paper.'

It was the piece of paper on which Booth had made his note, and which he had thrown angrily into the waste paper basket when Gruban had refused to agree to the commission, and which Gruban had later picked out and kept. Booth turned the paper over and over again, and as he did so Hastings read out the words written on it: 'Full ten per cent to F.H.B. Say £600 or £650.'

'Who is F.H.B.?' said Hastings.

The answer was, 'I know only one, myself.'

'What was the ten per cent on?'

'I do not know.'

'What was the amount of the Birmingham contract?'

'Six thousand pounds.'

Booth tried to make some explanations but in the first few minutes Hastings had shaken his confidence profoundly. Immediately Hastings struck again with another document to support him.

'Mr Booth,' he said, 'did you boast to Mr Gruban about your friendship with members of the Cabinet and how you could influence them?'

To which Booth answered, 'Whilst I know members of the Cabinet, I deny that I ever told Gruban that I could *influence* them.'

'Then', said Hastings, 'what about this telegram you sent to Gruban? "Portfolio received today. Have already spoken to Cabinet Minister and high official has called on me, so am hoping for good results."'

Booth then suggested that the use of the words 'Cabinet Minister' was a slip, to which Hastings responded rather grimly: 'Slip! I suggest it was a lie.' So the cross-examination continued and was utterly merciless.

In the result the jury awarded the plaintiff £4,750, and Hastings had taken a great step forward on the road that was to lead him to the heights.

I saw him scores and scores of times in later years, sitting in the front row with him and watching him more critically perhaps as his opponent; but he never did anything better than this great cross-examination of Handel Booth. He was at his very best – relentless, ruthless, eager, vehement, scornful, satirical, contemptuous, by turns – and it is no exaggeration at all to say that he simply destroyed Handel Booth.

When I recall that day and other days, I think principally of the wonderful animation he always displayed. He always seemed so alert, so alive, and the vehemence of his questions at times was quite overwhelming. The expressions on his face as he put his questions were all intended to be observed by the jury, and they added great force to his words. Hastings had mastered one simple but invaluable method of advocacy, and that was to be quite independent of the written brief. He had got it all into his head, and he could stand before the jury and ask his questions and deal with any answers from any quarter, whether from witness, jury, or judge, without referring to any documents and without distracting attention from the immediate purpose he had in his mind. Hastings had learned, too, what an immense advantage it is to the advocate to stand up straight and to be still. He very rarely gestured with his hands, and he had none of those irritating little habits such as fiddling with the tape on the brief or things of that kind. Serjeant Sullivan, I remember, used to drive his opponents to despair during a protracted trial by constantly tying and untying the tape on his brief or, what was much worse, by jingling the coins in his trouser pocket incessantly. Hastings never took his eyes off the jury when he was addressing them and he never stopped to sip water from a tumbler or to break in any way his concentration; and he managed at all times to convey the impression that he was in earnest, and was not simply playing a part. The importance of this cannot be over-estimated and, of course, it was part of the equipment of Hastings the advocate, who well knew its value. He had a good clear voice, and he always spoke so that he could be heard. He used simple language and avoided tortuous sentences. Like all great advocates, he seemed to divine what was going on in the minds of the jury and spoke to them as though he was one of them. He never flattered them or lectured them or tried to cajole them; but he *watched* them and studied them with infinite care, and made them feel, no doubt, that he respected their independence and their judgment. When he was examining his own witness to get his case before the jury, where the rules about the form of the questions that may be put are very strict, Hastings would conduct the examination as though it was a spontaneous conversation. He had one endearing habit which I came to know quite well. He would smile at some answer as though it had come to him as a surprise when it was in truth the answer he wanted and expected and which he had used all his skill to obtain. When the occasion demanded it, he could laugh a case out of court as well as any man I ever knew.

His sense of humour was sometimes a little different from that of the ordinary man, but in court he always used it with restraint and good sense. One of his more amusing cases was when a stockbroker with the unusual name of Blennerhassett brought an action for damages for libel because he had been held up to ridicule and contempt, as he alleged, in an illustrated advertisement for a children's game called 'Yo-Yo'. It was necessary for Mr Blennerhassett to prove that readers of the advertisement would reasonably think it referred to him. He therefore called a colleague from the Stock Exchange to prove this point, and the colleague was unwise enough to add that members of the Stock Exchange were not allowed to advertise, whereupon Hastings in cross-examination immediately produced this little gem of a question with an air of bland innocence: 'If you wanted to advertise yourself as a member of the Stock Exchange, would you select a picture of yourself being escorted to a mad-house playing with a Yo-Yo?' The court dissolved in laughter as Hastings intended and the judge finally ruled that there was no case to go to the jury.

But Hastings' great opportunity came to him in 1922, three years after he had been made a King's Counsel. And it came suddenly and unexpectedly. It is a fascinating thing to reflect upon that element in all life that men call luck or chance. In the profession of the law chance may bring the great opportunity to some men and deny it to others. Many men of great ability never get the opportunity to show their great qualities and either drift out of the profession as disappointed men or go through life with, as it were, a broken wing. I can never read without some emotion those verses of J. K. Stephen when he tells of the *Old School List*:

> There's a grave grey lawyer in King's Bench Walk
> Whose clients are passing few:
> He seldom speaks: in those lonely weeks
> What on earth can he find to do?
> Well he stroked the Eight – what a splendid fate! –
> And the Newcastle barely missed:
> A future Lord Chancellor, so we'd talk
> In the days of the Old School List.

But when the opportunity does come, as it came to Hastings, the great question then is: Can the man seize it and make the most of it? For in the profession of the law no words are so true as the words Brutus addresses to Cassius in *Julius Caesar*:

> There is a tide in the affairs of men,
> Which, taken at the flood, leads on to Fortune;
> Omitted, all the voyage of their lives
> Is bound in shallows and in miseries.

Hastings rose to the height of his great opportunity and never afterwards looked back.

The case was one in which a well-known racing journalist named Robert Sievier brought an action for libel against Richard Wootton, a well-known trainer of racehorses. Sievier was one of those flamboyant characters who manage to get a great public following to support them in whatever they do, whatever its nature. He was the owner of that famous St Leger winner, Sceptre, and at sixty years of age had behind him a varied kind of career

32

which would not stand a close and critical examination. He had been warned off the turf but had been reinstated and was still 'good old Bob' to his unthinking and admiring public. He edited a journal called the *Winning Post* and wrote a column under the heading 'Celebrities in Glass Houses', and in this column he attacked a wealthy South African racehorse owner, Mr Jack Joel. Joel had once got into trouble in South Africa about illicit diamond-buying, and Sievier was proposing to publish Joel's photograph between the photographs of two murderers. When Joel heard of this (as he was intended to do), he negotiated with Sievier through a man named Mills and agreed to pay Sievier £5,000 if he would not publish his (Joel's) photograph. At the same time he informed the police. Sievier was prosecuted for blackmail at the Old Bailey in 1908 and was defended by Rufus Isaacs who secured his acquittal. Through this same column Sievier had attacked Richard Wootton, accusing him of ordering his jockeys to pull their horses when Wootton had not backed them so that he could win on the horses he *had* backed. Wootton sued Sievier, but only got a farthing damages, the jury saying somewhat surprisingly that Sievier had acted without malice. Wootton nursed his grievances for a time and then published a pamphlet in which he called Sievier a swindler, a card-sharper, a thief, and a man with whom no decent person ought to associate. He set out many disgraceful episodes in Sievier's career, including the attempt to blackmail Mr Joel. Sievier then sued Wootton for libel. Upon the second day of the trial, just as the cross-examination of Sievier was beginning, Carson was called away to Ulster on political business; and the case was left in the hands of Hastings. It was the perfect kind of case for Patrick. The court was packed to overflowing, and Hastings was to conduct a hostile cross-examination with wonderful material for its effective use. I have already illustrated Hastings' methods in cases of fraud, and I use this case to illustrate his great skill in what is called re-examination. Sievier thought that, having been acquitted on the charge of blackmail, he was safe from attack on that score. But the Lord Chief Justice, the same Rufus Isaacs who had defended him in 1908 and was now Lord Reading, soon disillusioned him, saying that the present charge was one of libel, and if the defence was willing to raise the issue again, and take the risk of so doing, they were quite entitled to do so. Sievier then admitted that he *had* attacked Joel in the *Winning Post* and that he *had* received £5,000 from him through his friend Mills; there was no blackmail, he asserted: it was a loan as between friends. He actually challenged Hastings to put Mills into the witness-box, which Hastings, in fact, had long ago intended to do, and had Mills in court on subpoena. Now it must be understood that when counsel calls a witness for his own side he must not cross-examine him, and from the moment he went into the witness-box, it was clear that Mills had no intention of injuring Sievier if he could possibly help it. He said in answer to Hastings that he knew of the attacks on Joel, that he had handed Sievier a cheque for £5,000, but that the payment was a loan. Sievier, conducting his own case, now made the terrible mistake of cross-examining Mills, and Mills gladly responded, saying there never was any suggestion of blackmail, that Sievier had merely given him a letter to hand to Mr Joel thanking him for his kindness to Mills, and that he, Sievier, would not attack Joel again. This cross-examination gave Hastings the right to re-examine on any matters arising out of the cross-examination, and here is the perfect model of skill and restraint in carrying out that

34

task. The jury had listened to the tremendous cross-examination of Sievier which had lasted two days and had ranged over the whole of his life, and this short re-examination of Mills was the crowning touch. This is how it went:

'Did the Plaintiff show you any photographs to be incorporated with the proposed article on Mr Joel?'

'He did.'

'Whom did the photographs represent?'

'He said something about their being murderers.'

'Where were they to be placed?'

'One on each side of Mr Joel.'

'What for?'

'I do not know.'

'How could the publication be prevented?'

'If Joel paid £5,000.'

'Did Mr Joel hand you £5,000?'

'Yes.'

'What did you do with the money?'

'I handed it to Mr Sievier.'

'And was the publication stopped?'

'It was.'

In the end the jury returned a verdict for Mr Wootton, and Sievier left the court utterly discredited. Hastings in his later days of affluence, as Mr Montgomery Hyde records, was accustomed to say with feeling: 'When Carson went to Ulster that night he brought me fortune.'

I said earlier that Hastings was in some respects a law unto himself. In the trial of Mrs Barney for murder, when Hastings defended so brilliantly, Mr Justice Humphreys said of Patrick's closing speech that 'It was certainly one of the finest speeches that I ever heard at the Bar.' And yet there is nothing in that speech that seems to merit such high and unqualified praise. There is no distinction of language, no elegance of expression, merely a simple conversational narrative analysing the facts and making no attempt at passionate persuasion or anything like it. This is a part of the opening speech:

'Members of the Jury, there are cases in which advocates appearing for the defence are driven in despair to plead to the jury, and to urge that the defendant is entitled to the benefit of the doubt. I am not going to do anything of the sort. I am not going to ask you to give Mrs Barney the benefit of the doubt. I am going to show that there is no doubt and there is no evidence on which this woman could be convicted of any offence whatever.'

This was, to say the least of it, a very bold thing to say in the light of the evidence, particularly when a verdict of manslaughter was possible, but it was quite characteristic of Hastings. It was of course the old rhetorical device of Mark Antony declaiming over the dead body of Caesar, pretending to despise oratory and its persuasive effect, and yet at the same time indulging in it. And this is the peroration, if the word is not out of place:

'I am not going to beg for mercy and a lenient view of what has happened. I stand here, and I claim on the evidence Mrs Barney is entitled as of right to a verdict in her favour. She is a young woman with the whole of her life before her. I beg you to remember that. I ask you as a matter of justice and right that you should say "Not Guilty".'

There you have it – the cool and calm advocate, disdaining the forensic arts while brilliantly employing them. He captured the jury and the judge by an appeal to the head more than the heart and above all by the manner of his presentation.

Patrick Hastings, like Marshall Hall, remained at the Bar all his working life. He frequently said to me that he had no wish to be made a judge, and when I went to the Bench in 1941 he wrote me what I can only describe as a very sad letter, in which he said how much he would miss our battles together. But when he came to retire he wrote these words:

I sat back in the Lord Chief Justice's Court and I knew that I should never see that court again. . . . I could not very well complain. I had enjoyed a long innings and it was quite time for me to make way for younger men. Fate had not been unkind to me. I had climbed up a long steep road, and had managed to achieve a fair measure of success, and now was the time to go. After all it is better to leave from the top of the hill than to wait until you begin to slip down the other side.

It was bravely done and bravely spoken; and Patrick Hastings went to join the select company of those who made advocacy their calling and have brought honour to themselves and to their great profession.

SIR EDWARD CLARKE, K.C.

NOBODY will ever challenge the right of Edward Clarke to be ranked with the great advocates of the English Bar. In his day and generation, he was, in some respects, the greatest of them all. His outstanding gift was perfectly described in the great phrase of Tristram Shandy: 'Persuasion hung upon his lips.' In an age when advocacy was held in great esteem, nobody ever equalled Clarke in this marvellous persuasive power. Some of his learned brethren excelled him in some spheres. He lacked, for example, the overwhelming elemental force of Charles Russell and could not rival his incisive, persistent, penetrating power of cross-examination. Others perhaps had a greater sense of the dramatic or were more truly versatile; but Edward Clarke had the supreme gift – the advocate's pearl of great price – the gift of persuasion. This, when all is said and done, is the gift to which all other qualities of the advocate are subordinate; and it was by this gift that Clarke won his enduring fame.

When I write of Marshall Hall and Patrick Hastings, I write of men that I have known. I have seen them in their great moments in the courts, and I can see them still in all their grace and strength. But Edward Clarke I never saw in action. His career at the Bar ended before mine had properly begun. But whenever members of the Bar who had seen him in his great cases met together, at the Inns of Court or in the Bar Messes on circuit, and the talk turned on the great figures at the Bar, it was Clarke who lived in the memory and imagination. Men spoke of him with a kind of admiring wonder – 'Ah! but you should have heard Edward Clarke when he defended Adelaide

Bartlett' – just as though one of the great experiences of the world had been missed. I remember seeing him in the Inner Temple Hall in 1930 when he was nearing his nine-tieth birthday, and I looked upon him with veneration as I recalled the splendours and the triumphs of those wonderful fifty years at the Bar. And if I cannot give a first-hand impression of my own, I am fortunate in this: that the late Lord Maugham when he had become Lord, Chancellor, recorded *his* first sight of Edward Clarke in the courts. He had gone across Carey Street from Chancery chambers, where he was a pupil, to see if he could find, as he said, 'something more animated and human in the law in the King's Bench Division'. He certainly found it, for he saw Edward Clarke addressing a jury and this is how he described that memorable moment:

I was unable to drag myself away. Never had I heard such incomparable lucidity. Since that distant day I have listened to and admired all the great advocates of the English Bar . . . but no one that I ever heard surpassed Edward Clarke in the art of holding a jury. . . . Of all the aptitudes and abilities which together make up the complete forensic advocate, Edward Clarke, in ample measure, possessed them all.

It is foolish, and a little ungracious, to compare the advocates of one age with those of another, for the great advocate is the product of the age in which he happens to live and work. His first and all-important conquest must be the conquest of his contemporaries; and so completely did Edward Clarke make this conquest that, as can be seen in the tribute of Lord Maugham, his name and fame survive not only as an advocate of dazzling gifts, pre-eminent in persuasion, but as a great man in his own right, and as a truly Eminent Victorian.

Edward Clarke was born so long ago as 1841 and he

embodied many of the Victorian virtues together with some of their limitations. He believed in self-help and in material success. He believed in himself and in what education could do for him to help him to make his way in the world. His career was the kind that appealed particularly to the Victorian age, and indeed in all ages it has had a special fascination for the British people; for Edward Clarke was a striking example of the way a man can rise to fame and honour against great odds, largely by his own exertions. At the age of thirteen, Clarke was helping his father in a silversmith's shop in London, and his schooldays were over. But from then on he was cultivating his early and invincible love of reading, attending evening classes, taking the examinations of the Society of Arts and the outside examinations of Oxford University, practising his speeches at the local debating society, and generally making his own opportunities. He had no money, no influential friends, no connexion with the law, and no social standing, and his fixed determination to be called to the Bar showed his courage and his quality.

But Edward Clarke had possessions of another and much more valuable kind. He was full of energy and was not afraid of work. He had a wonderful memory, the gift of eloquence of a rare and valuable kind, and a sense of purpose that could not be moved or beaten down or disheartened. But beyond all other things – and this is the secret of Edward Clarke's tremendous career – he had that inward urge, born in the secret places of the heart, to excel, to triumph over his circumstances, and to become a famous and a distinguished man. It is not for me to explain the origin of this inward urge – some people no doubt would call it mere ambition – but with Edward Clarke it was like the seed which germinates and thrusts relentlessly, so that finally nothing in the world can stand against it.

But Edward Clarke's early ambition was not merely to have a career in the law. This was but a step to greater things. What he really wanted was a great political career and the law was merely the avenue by which a poor man might achieve it. Sir John Simon, afterwards Lord Simon, held the same view and expressed it publicly on many occasions. To the members of the Canadian Bar Association he said:

'I have never rated the practice of the law as falling within the higher ranges of human achievement. . . . A man who feels the urge to do his best in public life may get his chance by being a lawyer. Advocacy as practised at the Bar is just a way of earning a living; and a man's livelihood ought not to be the whole of a man's life.'

For Edward Clarke, the alluring prospect was *political* fame and power. He was a passionate admirer of Disraeli, and it was reading Disraeli's novels *Coningsby* and *Sybil* that first fired his political ambitions; but it was a chance visit to the House of Lords that really set him alight, with ambition to outsoar the circumscribed sphere of the law and to win fame in a wider world. Sir Winston Churchill, ever the great phrase-maker, once referred to the 'sharp agate points on which the ponderous balance of destiny turns'; and that afternoon in the gallery of the House of Lords was surely the great turning-point in the life of Edward Clarke. For it so happened that the aged Lord Lyndhurst, the former Lord Chancellor, intervened in the debate. The extraordinary deference shown by the House of Lords to Lyndhurst was impressive in the extreme, and the youthful, ambitious Edward Clarke was not only impressed – he was quite overcome. He knew from his reading that Lyndhurst had risen to his commanding position by his own exertions, and he was supremely confident that he could do the same. Lyndhurst had once said: 'What is wanted for success at the Bar is a clear head, a good memory, strong common sense and an aptitude for analysis and arrangement. Before these combined qualities, the difficulties of law vanish like the morning mist before the sun.'

Edward Clarke knew that he possessed all these things – and more. So, stimulated by the illustrious example of a man who, without wealth or social position, had reached the topmost heights of public life through the avenue of the law, he entered as a student at Lincoln's Inn in 1861 and was called to the Bar in 1864. He was then twenty-three years old and had already come a long way by his own industry and perseverance. For him, as it turned out, the real obstacles had been overcome. When once a start has been made at the Bar it is not difficult for a man of ability to make headway. It is the waiting period that tries men's souls. Edward Clarke got a quick start with small criminal cases at the London Sessions, and two of those small cases may be mentioned in passing, just to illustrate the immense changes in our way of life and in our criminal procedure since that far-away age of Edward Clarke. In 1866 he appeared at the Old Bailey to defend a man who was charged with furious driving down the Waterloo Road at a speed of no less than twelve miles an hour; and at the same Sessions he prosecuted a boy of eighteen on a charge of stealing five shillings and sixpence, for which the boy received a savage sentence of seven years' penal servitude.

The case which made his name known throughout the land and started him out on his brilliant career in the law was the case of Harriet Staunton, sometimes called the Penge Mystery. He was briefed for the defence of

Patrick Staunton on a charge of wilful murder. The year was 1877, when Clarke had been thirteen years at the Bar and was thirty-six years old. He had still before him thirty-seven more years at the Bar, to be filled with famous and sensational cases, some of which have become part of our social and national history. Thus, in 1886 he defended Adelaide Bartlett on a charge of murdering her husband by the administration of chloroform, one of those rare cases when advocacy can turn the scale. He won a verdict of not guilty by that quality of persuasion of which I have spoken; and, in my belief, no other counsel in England at that time could have done it. In 1890 he appeared in the Parnell Divorce suit. In 1891 he fought a most courageous fight for the plaintiff in the notorious Baccarat Case when the Prince of Wales gave evidence and was questioned by a member of the jury with great effect. In 1895 he appeared for Oscar Wilde in those three intensely dramatic trials at the Old Bailey. And in 1896 he appeared for Dr Jameson, who was prosecuted in London after the Jameson Raid in South Africa. He fought many battles for the brilliant and eccentric Mr Labouchère. But in the case of Harriet Staunton he was to lay the sure foundation for all his subsequent triumphs and to establish his title to be numbered with the great advocates. The future was hidden from him, as it is mercifully hidden from us all, but everything conspired to make the case of the Stauntons the first great milestone on the highway to wealth and fame.

The essence of the Staunton Case in the public mind was that a woman of weak intellect had been done to death by her callous husband and his relatives, by means of starvation and hideous neglect, in order to filch her small inheritance. The interest of the public can be described only as feverish, and the persons accused were never given a chance in public opinion. It must be added with regret that they were never given a chance by the judge at the trial, Mr Justice Hawkins. Edward Clarke permitted himself to say of Hawkins at a later date that 'he had no notion of what justice meant or of the obligations of truth and fairness'.

Harriet Staunton was a woman of thirty-five married to Louis Staunton, a young man of twenty-three. She possessed £2,000 and a further £2,000 in a reversionary interest under a will. Harriet's mother, with an instinctive dislike of Louis Staunton, tried unsuccessfully to have Harriet declared to be of unsound mind and to have her money protected by the Court of Chancery. As the law then stood, all Harriet's property passed to her husband. The mother was allowed to see Harriet only once after the marriage and was then rudely told by the husband never to try to see her again. In the year following the marriage Harriet gave birth to a son, and during her confinement a pretty young girl of eighteen, Alice Rhodes, whose sister was married to Patrick Staunton, the brother of Louis, came to live in the house. Harriet soon learnt that Louis Staunton and Alice Rhodes were living together. When she protested she was sent with her small son to the house of the brother Patrick in the village of Cudham in Kent. A little later, Louis Staunton and Alice Rhodes, now openly living together, came to live at the same village of Cudham in a house quite near to the house of Patrick. Louis took Harriet to London to sign a Deed disposing of her reversionary interest, and that was the very last appearance Harriet made in the outside world. The remainder of her life, about nine months, was spent in the house of Patrick Staunton, who was paid a pound a week for keeping her. Harriet's mother, learning that she was at the house of Patrick, called there to see her but was not allowed to do so. She went to the nearby house of Louis but was simply hustled from the door. She informed the police who watched the house of Louis, but without result, for Harriet was at the house of Patrick. Then Harriet's little boy was taken to Guy's Hospital and died there on the night of his entry. Four days later, Louis and Mrs Patrick Staunton reserved lodgings at Forbes Road, Penge, for a lady, 'inclined to be paralysed', as they said. That night the four Stauntons with Alice Rhodes went to Forbes Road, Penge. Harriet was speechless and barely conscious. She died about noon the next day. She had been seen by a doctor who gave a certificate of death, and in the ordinary way that might have been the end of the matter.

But fate moves in remarkable and mysterious ways. It so happened that a man, with the singular name of Casabianca, went into a shop on the corner of Forbes Road, and while he was there a young man (who turned out to be Louis Staunton) came into the shop to inquire where a death which had taken place that afternoon ought to be registered. When the young man went on to say, without any special reason for it, that the lady whose death was to be registered had been brought from the village of Cudham, Mr Casabianca was keenly interested at once. For he was Harriet's brother-in-law, and Cudham was the place where Harriet's mother had been so rudely rebuffed. Mr Casabianca went to the police next morning and asked for inquiries to be made. The certificate of death was withdrawn, and an inquest was ordered. Four doctors conducted a post-mortem examination and certified that death was due to starvation. A very terrifying state of things was disclosed. The body was fearfully dirty and dreadfully emaciated. The full disclosures at the inquest inflamed local feeling against the Stauntons to a burning passion of resentment, and in consequence the trial was removed to the Old Bailey. Edward Clarke was briefed for Patrick Staunton; Montagu Williams, a famous criminal defender, for Louis Staunton; Douglas Straight for Mrs Patrick Staunton; and Percy Gye for Alice Rhodes.

The whole case was to turn on the medical evidence and it was agreed by defending counsel that this part of the case should be left to Edward Clarke. Two famous doctors were of the opinion that death was *not* due to starvation but to tubercular meningitis or Addison's disease. Unfortunately there was no mention of this at the time of the death, and the tests which would have established or disproved this view were never made. The public interest in the case had grown enormously and the two critical questions now were 'was death due to starvation or to some other cause' and 'had Harriet Staunton been treated by the accused in the way that people would have treated her who desired to see her die?'

It must be remembered that at that time the prisoners were not allowed to give evidence themselves. That was not permitted until the Criminal Evidence Act of 1898, and the only evidence for the defence that could be given was the evidence of the two doctors who attributed the death to disease and not to starvation. Everything, therefore, turned on the speeches of counsel, and Clarke's speech is universally considered to have been a masterpiece of persuasive eloquence. I have said before that to read an advocate's speech, when the circumstances which called it forth have long passed away, is to make the reader wonder whether the magic or the power could ever have been there; but Clarke himself said of this speech that it more nearly realized his ideal of what a closing speech should be than any other speech he ever made at any other time. It was made in a court where the question uppermost in every mind was whether these four people were destined for the gallows, and the public outside the court were gripped by the same question. The argument on the facts and the medical evidence had been long and detailed and then came the wonderful voice of Edward Clarke making its last appeal. This was its conclusion:

'Gentlemen of the Jury, human justice is depicted as blind. It is not given to human justice to see and to know, as the great Eternal knows, the thoughts and feelings and actions of all men. She has to depend on what she hears. She must depend upon inferences. She must depend upon testimony. How should she deal with the irrevocable issues of life and death unless those recollections are exact, that testimony trustworthy, those inferences uncontradicted? How should she lift the sword to strike – and you gentlemen guide her hand today – while, at the moment the accusing voice is in her ear denouncing the crime, the echo of that very voice is heard proclaiming that the prisoners are innocent, and passionless science steps to her side to warn her that there may in truth have been no crime committed.'

The Attorney General, for the Crown, went out of his way to pay tribute to Edward Clarke's speech, but it had no effect whatever upon Mr Justice Hawkins. He spent the whole of the next day in summing-up and in terms which were deadly to the defence and which were intended to be so. It was after ten o'clock at night when he finished, and shortly after eleven o'clock when the jury returned with a verdict of Guilty against all the prisoners. It was a terrible moment. Mr J. B. Atlay, who edited the account of the trial in the Notable British Trials series, said of it:

The scene while a man and, worse still, a woman receives sentence of death is solemn and eerie enough in any circumstances. But when morning has slowly worn away to evening, to the accompaniment of a single, steady unfaltering voice, until flickering candle or flaming gaslight add their quota to the tainted air, the strain on the least responsive spectator becomes almost unendurable.

Patrick Staunton put his hand into that of his wife in an effort to comfort her in that most bitter moment. Louis Staunton and Alice Rhodes seemed to have no thought for each other and, quite overwhelmed with terror, gazed unseeingly at the judge in his black cap in the ghostly light. Hawkins sentenced them all to death in words of the utmost severity. But Edward Clarke's efforts were far from being in vain. Although the jury had no doubt been powerfully influenced by the judge in giving their verdict, Clarke's appeal had had a very great effect in the country. Over four hundred doctors with the famous Sir William Jenner at their head had signed a declaration saying that the evidence of the post-mortem examination showed the cause of death to be injury to the membranes of the brain and not starvation, and Charles Reade, the famous author of *The Cloister and the Hearth*, published some very pungent and destructive criticism of the trial. In the result, all the prisoners were reprieved and Alice Rhodes was released. Patrick Staunton died in prison soon after the trial, and Mrs Patrick Staunton was soon released too.

The case had raised Edward Clarke to the very front rank as an advocate and, from now on, the early ambition to seek political fame was abandoned for the desire to win and retain a great legal reputation. This was advanced by many cases but most notably by Clarke's defence of Adelaide Bartlett in 1886. She was charged with the murder of her husband, and Clarke believed her to be innocent. But because of that belief, a legend grew up that Edward Clarke never defended anybody unless he believed them to be innocent, and that his advocacy never touched the heights unless he was able to entertain that belief. This is really quite unjust and is completely refuted by his most admirable and splendid conduct in the case of Oscar Wilde. It is not the business of counsel to decide whether people are guilty or not, and the belief that counsel fights hardest when he believes his client to be innocent will not bear examination. When Edward Clarke defended Oscar Wilde at the Old Bailey on the criminal charges, he knew for a certainty that Wilde was guilty. A greater advocate even than Edward Clarke, the great Erskine, had said to the jury when defending Tom Paine:

'If the advocate refuses to defend from what he may think of the charge or the defence, he assumes the character of the judge, nay, he assumes it before the hour of judgement . . . and puts the heavy influence of a perhaps mistaken opinion into the scale against the accused. . . .'

Before he accepted the brief to appear for Wilde on the first occasion, when Wilde was the Prosecutor and the Marquess of Queensbury the defendant, the charge against the defendant being criminal libel for most serious allegations made against the moral character of Oscar Wilde, Clarke said to Wilde in the presence of his solicitor, 'I can only accept this Brief, Mr Wilde, if you can assure me, on your honour as an English gentleman, that there is not and never has been any foundation for the charges the Marquess of Queensbury makes against you.' Wilde stood up and solemnly assured Clarke that the charges were absolutely false and groundless. Of course, Clarke could not have asked that question if he had been invited to accept the brief in a *criminal* case. Wilde told Clarke a lie. But on the second day of the trial, while Wilde was still being cross-examined by Carson, Wilde came up to Clarke at the adjournment and said, 'Can they examine me about anything and everything they choose?' and when Clarke said 'Yes', Wilde said, 'Can they ask about an incident that has never yet been mentioned?' When Clarke said, 'Certainly, but what is it that is on your mind?' Wilde said to Clarke: 'Well, sometime ago I was turned out of the Albemarle Hotel in the middle of the night and a boy was with me. It might be awkward if they found out.' Clarke had been very uneasy during Carson's cross-examination, and he was now certain that Wilde had deceived him. He spent an anxious night considering the new situation, and next morning he told Wilde that the result of the case would almost certainly be the acquittal of Queensbury and Wilde's arrest. He got Wilde's consent to withdraw the prosecution and told him that there was no need for him to be present when the announcement was made in court, intending that Wilde should take the opportunity of escaping from the country. Instead of doing that, Wilde spent the afternoon in various hotels, and was arrested that very night. Nevertheless, Clarke wrote at once to Wilde's solicitor, offering to defend Wilde if he wished it, without fee or reward. Clarke made a great fight and came very near to success; but he fought all the way with the knowledge in his own mind that Wilde was guilty.

Clarke knew that the art of advocacy was beset with perils of a very special kind and knew also that the disfavour in which the advocate is sometimes held is due to a grave misconception of the advocate's true function. The advocate does not profess to present his own views or his own beliefs; he is there to say for the man charged all that the man could say for himself were he able to do so. Clarke was a splendid example of public duty and private faithfulness. He retired after fifty years at the Bar without the political distinction to which he had once aspired and without the high judicial office to which his ambition later turned, although in 1897 he had refused the great office of Master of the Rolls.

Many great advocates at the close of their careers, when no judicial preferment has come their way, have expressed regret that they are leaving nothing permanent behind them. But Edward Clarke was not of their company. He carried with him into his retirement the esteem of all his brethren of the Bench and Bar, eloquently voiced by Sir John Simon, as Attorney General, at a great farewell dinner of the Bench and Bar, when he said of Clarke:

'He so conducted himself in the discharge of his professional duty that he set to every one of us the example of how a man may devote himself unsparingly to the cause he has to advocate, and yet remain in some sense a minister of justice.'

And it was entirely fitting that on that splendid occasion, Edward Clarke, surrounded by famous judges and counsel, should say bravely and proudly, as his parting message to his friends:

'And so it comes to pass that at the end of fifty years I finish as I began, as a private member of the English Bar. To some that will look like failure . . . but there has been no failure and I have no reproaches or regrets. If success in life is to be measured in terms of personal happiness, as I think it ought to be, then no man ever had a more successful life than mine . . . for I have spent my life in the practice of the most interesting profession in the world.'

SIR RUFUS ISAACS, K.C.

IT is now nearly fifty years since Rufus Isaacs became Lord Chief Justice of England. That great office, dating back to the Norman Conquest, is thought by many to be the richest prize of the legal world; and Rufus Isaacs gained it within twenty-six years of his call to the Bar. I have a very special reason to remember him. As a very inexperienced junior counsel I had come up to London from Birmingham, where I then practised, to argue a small case in the Court of Criminal Appeal. That court is normally composed of three judges, presided over by the Lord Chief Justice, and they sit in the largest court in the Strand in all the majesty of their scarlet and ermine. This was my first appearance there and, coming from Birmingham as I did, I knew nobody in the court and felt most dreadfully alone. I was a little over-awed by the solemnity and splendour of my new surroundings, and the very last thought in my head was that one day I should sit where these men like gods were now sitting. But what really captured my imagination was the sight of Rufus Isaacs, the new Lord Chief Justice and Lord Reading. He looked dignified and self-possessed sitting there with his handsome acquiline face; and when he spoke his voice was deep and resonant and most memorable. When my appeal was over and he delivered the judgment of the court, he went out of his way to say a few words of encouragement to me, with a kindly smile and a courteous inclination of the head. I was quite overcome, but I knew then what charm of manner and courtesy can do to win allegiance, and also what a kindly word from the Bench can do to help the beginner at the start of his hard and difficult journey – and I hope I have never forgotten it.

But in the twenty-six years he spent at the Bar, Rufus Isaacs was the chief figure in many memorable trials, and in many more he shared the honours with his great friend and rival, Sir Edward Carson. People still remember the tragic downfall of Whittaker Wright in 1904, the inquiry into the loss of the *Titanic* on her maiden voyage in 1912, and the most memorable trial of Frederick Seddon for the murder of Miss Barrow in 1912, when Rufus Isaacs and Marshall Hall met in one of the very greatest forensic contests of our history, so full of that peculiar human interest which belongs to the Courts of Law.

Comparing Rufus Isaacs with other great advocates, I have come to the conclusion that he is the most outstanding example I know of the glittering rewards that success in the courts can bring. I do not mean the very large income that Rufus Isaacs made; though in that respect I doubt whether many ever made quite so much money as he did at the Bar. But his rewards were much greater than mere money, and they all came because he had first won a great name for himself as an advocate. Lady Oxford is credited with the saying that Rufus Isaacs was one of the most ambitious men she ever knew, but to all outward seeming he was the least ambitious of men. Lord Simon, who knew him intimately, said that in 1912, when Lord Haldane was made Lord Chancellor, Rufus Isaacs was deeply hurt because he was passed over, he then being Attorney General and only fifty-one years old. Had he been made Lord Chancellor, it would have been on the footing that there were no more worlds to conquer; for nobody had the smallest idea then of the dazzling preferments that time and a great European war would bring. His ambition would seem to have ended there.

When Rufus Isaacs was called to the Bar in 1887 he showed no overmastering desire to achieve fame in the law, or fame in public life. The Bar was in fact his second choice of a profession after an ignominious failure in his first. He had been unable to meet his obligations on the Stock Exchange, was hammered, and had perforce to abandon that vocation. In that desperate moment the uppermost thought in his mind was to go to America to start a new life, without any very clear idea of what that new life might be. He became a lawyer because his mother came to him and besought him not to cut himself off from his friends, and said that if he desired to go to the Bar his parents would help him to do so. So they did, and it may seem a very strange thing to say, but the great offices subsequently filled by Rufus Isaacs, Solicitor General, Attorney General, Lord Chief Justice of England, Ambassador to the United States, Viceroy of India, Foreign Secretary, all came to him because he had first shown his remarkable gifts as an advocate in the Courts of Law. He was not one of the great parliamentarians: John Simon said he never gained the ear of the House of Commons; he was not a great platform orator like Lloyd-George or F. E. Smith; but he was made Solicitor General in 1910 because of his pre-eminent position at the Bar and from that first appointment all other things flowed. Already legends have gathered about his name, the chief being that he ran away from school to be the cabin boy in a small ship which was making a voyage to India, where one day, forty-four years later, he was to return in all the pomp and splendour of the Viceroy. This is not quite true, but it has enough truth to allow the romantic-minded to think of Rufus Isaacs as the poor cabin boy who rose to be Viceroy.

Rufus Isaacs, who was born in London in 1860, was in

fact the son of well-to-do parents, who sent him to a Jewish preparatory school and other schools in Brussels, London, and Hanover. But because of his setback on the Stock Exchange, he was twenty-seven years old when he was called to the Bar. To be called to the Bar later than most men is not the great disadvantage it is sometimes said to be. On the contrary, men with a little experience of life, such as Rufus Isaacs at twenty-seven and Douglas Hogg at thirty, have shown conclusively what an advantage a little training of the right kind can be. Although Rufus Isaacs was without public-school or university experience, he knew something of commerce, and with his natural aptitude for figures he made headway at once. Most men spend long years in county courts and magistrates' courts, at Sessions and Assizes in the country, slowly building up their practice; but Rufus Isaacs rarely left London and after the first five years his practice was almost entirely in the High Court. He became a Queen's Counsel in 1898 and Marshall Hall took silk at the same time. Unlike some juniors whose successful application for silk can ruin them because they find themselves unable to sustain competition with the best brains at the Bar, Rufus Isaacs had every qualification for the front row and was very soon to show it. In the six years that followed his taking silk he was engaged in many cases that brought his name prominently before the public, some of which are now forgotten, but some have shaped and fashioned the law as it is applied in the courts today. The greatness of Rufus Isaacs is shown by his amazing versatility and his

supreme skill in every kind of case in which he was engaged. I have already confessed the difficulty of conveying a true impression of a famous advocate of the past by recalling the occasions of his skill and mastery. But there are three cases of Rufus Isaacs that never seem to lose their power over the imagination, and the first of them was the trial of Whittaker Wright in 1904.

Isaacs had only been a silk for six years when he was called upon to prosecute this great financier, who was a most remarkable man by any view, and one who had completely captured the public imagination. He had started from nothing and by the time he was thirty he was, largely through speculation in America, a very rich man. He came back to England and was soon involved in vast financial transactions. The members of the public were quite enthralled. They tumbled over each other to subscribe for his shares, and he presented to the world a tremendously impressive figure of solid prosperity on an enormous scale. He was regarded as the modern Midas, the legendary king who had wished that anything he touched might become gold and had had his wish granted. He had all the outward trappings of great wealth: the gorgeous mansion in Park Lane, the quite fabulous country mansion at Godalming with its priceless furniture and fittings, its woods and lakes, and a great army of workmen continually at work building and creating a palace of extreme and extravagant luxury. But in 1900 the incredible thing happened. He was unable to meet his obligations, despite all his manipulations and manoeuvring, and all his vast empire was suddenly in utter ruin. Thousands were ruined with him and many members of the Stock Exchange were among them. The authorities seemed reluctant to prosecute, but the angry stockbrokers obtained an order from a Chancery judge sanctioning a prosecution for publishing false balance sheets, knowing them to be false, with intent to defraud. But by that time Whittaker Wright had fled the country and there were great difficulties over his extradition, so that it was 1904 before the trial came on before Mr Justice Bigham and a jury.

Rufus Isaacs prosecuted for the stockbrokers and described the case as one of extreme complexity, as indeed it was. It was so complicated that when Mr Justice Bigham was asked to give the jury an abstract of the twenty-four counts in the Indictment he said, 'I might as well give the jury the *Encyclopaedia Britannica*'. The case was tried at the Law Courts in the Strand in order to have a special jury, and this was to have tragic consequences, because prisoners are searched before trial at the Old Bailey, but that was not done at the Law Courts. Rufus Isaacs spoke for five hours in explaining the case to the jury. When the evidence was called, his mastery of every detail was clearly seen and he steered his way through the astonishing complications with unruffled ease, to the admiration of everybody who watched him. This was advocacy of a very rare and special kind, seen at its best in the grasp of detail combined with the superlative gift of explaining complicated figures with complete lucidity to lay minds. It was not a case for eloquence; it was a case for patient exposition in plain speech. Whittaker Wright went into the witness-box when the trial had lasted more than a week and he soon showed that he, too, was the master of every detail. Men watched the duel between Isaacs and Whittaker Wright with a kind of spellbound admiration for both witness and counsel. But Isaacs quite relentlessly broke through every defence of Whittaker Wright and when he left the witness-box he was a broken and ruined man – and knew it. As though he had anticipated the verdict and the sentence of seven years' Penal Servitude, he had scribbled the roman numeral VII on the writing pad he had used, seven years being the maximum sentence the Statute laid down for his offence. When he was taken to the room he had been using at the Courts he thanked all who had helped him at the trial, and then in the act of lighting a cigar he suddenly fell to the ground, and in a moment he was dead. He had taken cyanide of potassium and had apparently had the tablet at the back of his mouth throughout the day's events.

The magnificent conduct of the case, the superb cross-examination of the great financier, the masterly grasp of the most complicated facts, the lucidity with which he explained the case to the jury – all these things placed Rufus Isaacs at the very summit of his profession. He was then only forty-three years old. There were more worlds to conquer but in truth the main battle had been won in sixteen years. It was not, of course, to be 'roses, roses all the way', for the lamentable Marconi episode in 1912 was yet to come; but Rufus Isaacs was to go on to undreamt-of triumphs. To Lord Simon, who agreed with Mr Balfour that the charges of corruption against Isaacs in the Marconi episode were futile and absurd from the beginning and unworthy of the consideration of the House of Commons, the case was surprising because so wise an adviser of others as was Isaacs failed to see that, when wrongly accused of an improper transaction, he ought to have said how the confusion had arisen. It was simple enough. The English Marconi Company had contracts with the British Government for the equipment of wireless stations, and the brother of Rufus Isaacs was the Chairman of the Company. There was an *American* Marconi Company but it had no interest whatever in the English Company. Persuaded by his brother, Rufus Isaacs bought some *American* Marconi shares, and when malicious rumours were spread that he had bought *English* Marconi Company shares he made a statement in the House of Commons denying any such purchase, but said nothing about the *American* Marconi shares. When Isaacs told Simon the facts immediately after his first statement in the House of Commons, Simon besought him to make a supplementary statement the next day, but it was not done and a terrible price had to be paid.

In the year 1904 Rufus Isaacs became the Liberal Member for Reading and there is no doubt that his victory was due in some measure to the fact that he was already a national figure because of his prowess in the courts of law. It was an example of the law once more providing the avenue to public life and work. But election to Parliament meant no cessation in the long line of famous cases. In 1905 there was one case on which Rufus Isaacs prided himself, and with good reason. It was the defence of Sir Edward Russell, afterwards the first Lord Russell of Liverpool and the editor of a great Liberal paper, the *Liverpool Daily Post*. Although the case took place long before I was called to the Bar, I remember it very well. In the north-country town where I was born it was followed with absorbing interest, and I can recall the excitement of it down to this day.

Sir Edward Russell had attacked the members of the Licensing Committee of the Liverpool Justices, because he said that they were not really trying to reduce the number of public houses in Liverpool as the Licensing Act of 1904 allowed, and added that it was only what was to be expected of the friends of the liquor trade. The eight Conservative members of the Committee considered this to be a reflection on their personal honour, and rather hastily, and very unwisely, decided to prosecute Sir Edward in the criminal courts for criminal libel. The proceedings were by way of a Criminal Information which took the place of an Indictment and did away with the preliminaries in the magistrates' courts, so the first hearing of the case was at the Liverpool Assizes in St George's Hall.

In Liverpool and the North Country in particular, the announcement of these criminal proceedings came with a tremendous shock. To think of so distinguished a man as Russell on a criminal charge at the Assizes simply staggered the imagination. It was the topic on every tongue. Excitement rose to tremendous heights. Russell pleaded not guilty and said that the alleged libel was true and published in the public interest and that there was no imputation of corrupt or dishonest motives. The trial lasted for three days and was a resounding triumph for Rufus Isaacs. He regarded it as a great opportunity to vindicate the right of free speech and to vindicate it in one of the great Conservative strongholds. By a very adroit cross-examination, he elicited the fact that the whole of the proceedings of the Licensing Committee were conducted on party lines, and also obtained a most valuable admission from Sir Charles Petrie, one of the eight plaintiffs, that when he read the article he had not construed it as an imputation of corrupt or dishonest motives. When he opened the defence, in the presence of a crowded court, he made one of the finest speeches of his life, no doubt moved by the great theme of free speech, and the importance of the occasion. He opened on a confident and compelling note with all the charm of his melodious voice:

'I don't hesitate to say', he said, 'that not only was Sir Edward Russell entitled to make the observation contained in this article upon the action of these Licensing Justices in Liverpool, who were the predominant political party on this Committee, but that he was entitled to comment on the attitude of the judge on the Bench, and upon the action of all the magistrates in every court throughout the country. . . . Fox's Act established this one great principle, the fundamental principle of justice in this country: that the question whether an article is a libel is not to be decided by the judge however strong his views may be, but the question is to be decided . . . by the jury. This is the law of this free country, and you, gentlemen, are called upon to administer that law.'

He made another powerful speech after Sir Edward had given evidence, and Mr Justice Bray, who presided, said that he had never heard two finer speeches in his life. In his second speech Rufus Isaacs had the rare and satisfying experience of asking the jury to follow the view of one of the plaintiffs, Sir Charles Petrie, and the jury of Liverpool citizens did so. It is no wonder that the *Liverpool Daily Post* said next day:

And perhaps the greatest result . . . will be that the magnificient championship of Mr Rufus Isaacs, worthy of Erskine and Lord Russell of Killowen, acknowledged by the very Bench to have conferred distinction on the Northern Circuit and on the whole Bar, will arouse the press to a sense of its rights, and the country to a recognition of the services the press renders to the causes of reform.

I was twenty-one years old at the time and the advocacy of Rufus Isaacs made a powerful impression on me, and undoubtedly stirred some of those feelings which were ultimately to lead me to the Bar and the courts of law.

But the case by which Rufus Isaacs will be best remembered is the trial of Frederick Seddon and his wife on a charge of murdering their lodger, Miss Barrow, by the administration of arsenic. It was the case in which Marshall Hall made such a splendid defence, and, with Rufus Isaacs, then Attorney General, prosecuting for the Crown, the case became one of the most famous in our history, both for the manner in which it was conducted, and for the sustained interest the evidence aroused. There is no need to set out the facts in any detail, for they are well known; but there are one or two points of very special interest to me and to which I would like to draw attention.

Seddon was a most intelligent man but he was a miser and avaricious in the extreme. Fate so decreed that he took into his house as a lodger a sick and slightly mad old lady who was as avaricious and miserly as himself. She was also the possessor of a few thousand pounds' worth of property. When she died, only a year or so later, all her property was found to be in the hands of Seddon. He spent the smallest possible sum over her funeral, and wrangled over that, finally forcing a small commission of 12s. 6d. from the undertaker. He roused the suspicions of Miss Barrow's relatives by his behaviour, and the body of Miss Barrow was exhumed. It contained more than two grains of arsenic, which meant that at least five grains had been taken within two days of death, and that was a fatal dose. The all-important question at the trial was whether it could be proved that the Seddons had administered arsenic to Miss Barrow.

But *could it be proved?* The only source of arsenic suggested was in some fly-papers said to have been bought at a chemist's by Maggie Seddon, their sixteen-year-old daughter: but Marshall Hall blew the evidence of identification of Maggie by the chemist absolutely sky high. No other source was ever suggested. With the fly-paper evidence out of the way, Mrs Seddon had as much opportunity of administering the poison as her husband, and motive was not lacking on her part as well. Why then was Seddon convicted and Mrs Seddon acquitted? The answer most certainly is: because of the Criminal Evidence Act of 1898. That Act enabled Seddon to give evidence and he *wanted* to give evidence. It has been said that Marshall Hall was opposed to this course, but Seddon was a headstrong man and quite inordinately confident of his power to stand up to the cross-examination of Rufus Isaacs, the most brilliant cross-examiner of the day: and so he went into the box – and destroyed himself. It is quite clear that the Act of 1898 did not prove in practice the boon to prisoners it had been held out to be, and Seddon is the first name that leaps to the mind in this connexion. If he had not gone into the witness-box he *might* have been acquitted, because his guilt was not *proved*, and, as I have said, it was hard to differentiate where guilt lay between him and Mrs Seddon. My own view is that he would have been convicted in any event, but he made his conviction certain by going into the witness-box.

The cross-examination of Rufus Isaacs was as near perfection as can be imagined. Cool, calm, suave, incisive, searching, but never oppressive, conducting himself throughout with an unfailing courtesy, he allowed Seddon to show himself in his true character – a hard-bargaining, selfish, cruel, and money-loving man. The opening questions of the cross-examination have become as famous as the opening sentence of John Inglis, the Dean of Faculty, when defending Madeleine Smith. Inglis began with what has been called the perfect opening and has been quoted by many defending counsel since then. 'Gentlemen of the Jury,' he said, 'the charge against the prisoner is murder, and the punishment of murder is death; and that simple statement is sufficient to suggest to you the awful nature of the occasion which brings you and me face to face.'

Rufus Isaacs began: 'Mr Seddon' – observe the 'Mr', for it was used with intent, and with great effect – 'Mr Seddon,' said that calm, courteous voice, 'did Miss Barrow live with you from July 1910 till September 1911?'

'Yes,' said Seddon.

'Did you like her?'

It was almost too much for Seddon in its surprise and subtlety, and he could only repeat the question, 'Did I like her?' He couldn't say 'Yes' for the jury already knew the repellent character of Miss Barrow; he couldn't say 'No' for that might strengthen the motive for the poisoning; but he showed his acuteness of mind by saying: 'She wasn't a woman you could have been in love with, but I sympathized with her deeply.'

His cross-examination lasted six hours and the longer it lasted the clearer it became that Seddon was the murderer. It wasn't being proved by the Crown witnesses; it was being proved by Seddon himself. The jury were no longer troubled about where the arsenic was procured, or by whose hand it was administered. Poison was undoubtedly the cause of death, and Seddon had the opportunity to administer it. There was motive in the horrible greed revealed by the financial transactions, and to crown it all here was all Miss Barrow's little fortune in the hands of Seddon; and he had revealed himself as a callous monster. When he was questioned by Rufus Isaacs about having been seen counting out Miss Barrow's gold on the very afternoon of her death, he flared up with indignation, but could not forbear to add, 'I would have had all day to count the money', an answer which visibly tightened the coils about him. The evidence against Seddon was not overwhelming, but by his answers to cross-examination he showed plainly that he knew much more about the murder than he admitted; and the measure of the skill of Rufus Isaacs was that he led Seddon to convict himself. He led, and Seddon had to follow. Guilt can be led to bring itself out into the open as I discovered in 1931 when I had a similar experience with a man named Rouse.

Rufus Isaacs was soon to leave the Bar for the Bench, but notwithstanding all the glories and the triumphs that lay ahead of him in the legal and the political spheres, it is as a great advocate that he will be longest remembered; for there in the Courts – in the front row – was the source of his strength and the foundation of his most wonderful career.

SIR CHARLES RUSSELL, Q.C.

WHEN an advocate has been dead for sixty years, the 'iniquity of oblivion', as Sir Thomas Browne described it, has usually completed its work. But when men speak today of Charles Russell, who died in 1900, they almost always say 'the *great* Charles Russell' or 'the *famous* Lord Russell of Killowen'. No tribute to his memory could really be more eloquent than this; for Russell was one of those remarkable figures in the law who was equally great as an advocate and as a judge. Indeed, there are some discerning critics who hold the view that Charles Russell will be best remembered for his six memorable years as Lord Chief Justice of England, and that his immense fame as an advocate has tended to obscure his greatness as a judge. But the quality that made him great in both spheres was something quite distinct from the conventional things, such as training and aptitude or legal education; it was, to use a common expression, 'the way that he was made', the innate quality with which he was born, the nature of his forceful personality, which could dominate and overwhelm other men, whether they were jurymen, witnesses, or judges. He was once described by that great judge, Lord Bowen, as an 'elemental force' and the description, because it is true, has stuck to him ever since. In one of our best books of legal reminiscences, entitled *Pie Powder*, now unfortunately out of print, the learned author, Mr Foote K.C., said of Russell:

Russell was a great orator, a great man, and a great lawyer, but he was not in these respects superior to all others – not even to his own contemporaries. But as a great personality and an elemental force, Russell was more than pre-eminent – he was overwhelming.

In the intimate biography of Russell written by Mr Barry O'Brien, this opinion of Mr Foote is fully endorsed, and it was also the view expressed by Lord Justice Mathew in the *Dictionary of National Biography* when he said:

His extraordinary power when addressing a jury was owing not so much to any oratorical display as to the authority which he could always exercise over those he sought to influence. Spellbound under his vigorous and often passionate reasoning, their verdict was often due to the merits, not of the litigant, but of his counsel.

I emphasize this outstanding quality of Charles Russell at the outset, because it is the key to his character. It explains his supremacy at the Bar, and his commanding authority on the Bench. It explains, also, why in his early days at the English Bar, his style of advocacy was open to strong criticism and complaint. He was careless of the small matters that make life at the Bar tolerable and pleasant for those engaged in strenuous forensic contests, and was apt to be contemptuous of others. He was an Irishman with a quick temper, and there were many angry exchanges with opposing counsel, sometimes even with jurymen, and not infrequently with the judge himself. Nevertheless, he made no lasting enemies. As the years went by, he won universal admiration for his brilliance, and gained the affection of all because of his transparent honesty of purpose and the genuine kindness of his heart. But to the end he dominated by the sheer power of his personality, and that power was always the chief thing about him.

Charles Russell was born at Newry in Ireland in 1832, and after a very ordinary school life became a solicitor in

1854. He practised in Londonderry and Belfast, and very soon made his mark in the county courts by the vigour of his advocacy. He was not what we are accustomed to call 'a born orator', and he made himself the great speaker he became by taking infinite pains and by constant practice: except for the select few, it is the only way. It was the way followed by so great a man as Abraham Lincoln, who made the noblest short speech at Gettysburg that ever came from the lips of man. Russell was a strong Roman Catholic, and in his first year as a solicitor he made his name a household word in Ulster by his defence of the Catholic community in one of the villages of Antrim. A very violent attack was being made by a Protestant lecturer on the Catholic faith when a village woman threw a pail of water in his face. It seems very strange that an incident of that kind should affect the whole life and career of Charles Russell; but it did. He defended the woman when she was prosecuted for assault, and he displayed all those qualities that were to make the great Lord Coleridge say in later years: 'He is the biggest advocate of the century and the ablest man in Westminster Hall.' He overwhelmed the prosecutor by his passionate cross-examination; he withstood the attempted tyranny of the Bench; and he made a speech of singular beauty in which his love of Ireland and its people was perfectly expressed. His success in this case led all his friends to urge him to go to the English Bar, where there would be greater worlds to conquer and where his remarkable powers could find more adequate expression. When the judge at the Newry Quarter Sessions expressed the same view in most emphatic terms, he decided to take the great step, for he had long cherished the wish to be an advocate in the superior courts. Despite some family opposition, he came to England, entered as a student at

Lincoln's Inn, and was called to the English Bar in 1859 when he was twenty-seven years of age. Although he made his home in London, he practised mostly in Liverpool where there were many Irishmen, and quite soon he became widely known throughout the north of England. He appeared occasionally in the courts in London, notably on one occasion when he so impressed Lord Westbury, the Lord Chancellor, that he offered him a county court judgeship which Russell had the good sense to refuse. He had powerful rivals on the northern circuit but in time he outstripped them all. Sir John Holker, afterwards Lord Justice Holker, was his chief rival, and Russell himself thought that Holker was a better advocate than he was; but again the old comparison was made: 'Holker may be the better advocate, but Russell is the better man.' Charles Russell was what might be called the perfect all-rounder. He made his presence felt in any company he entered – in a court of law, on a racecourse, or in a card club. When he came into court he seemed to draw the interest of everybody in it. He had a splendid presence and a wonderful, piercing glance that could strike terror into the heart of a dishonest witness, and whatever he did, whether it was cross-examination or an address to the jury, he always seemed so impressive and convincing that he was almost irresistible.

Russell took infinite pains to be thoroughly prepared before he went into court and mastered the tiniest details so that when he was in court he could watch the jury and the judge, in everything they did, however trivial it might seem. Russell always regarded this as a matter of first importance. He possessed that quality of the great advocate which appreciates the significance and meaning of everything that goes on in court, whether it is some slight stir in the jury box, some surprising turn in the evidence, some word from the judge indicating a view, some action of his opponent, or some sudden change of expression on the face of a witness. He was in fact always on the alert and ready for everything. Moreover he was absolutely fearless. Just as he had withstood the magistrates on his first appearance for the defence at Belfast, so he would not hesitate for a moment to stand up to any judge and, if the need arose, to address the judge with vehemence, if he thought the rights of the advocate were being invaded. He once addressed some angry and rather violent words to Mr Justice Denman, who said he could not trust himself to reprove Russell that night because of his sorrow and resentment, but would adjourn the court and consider what to do next morning. But next morning when the learned judge began to refer to the 'painful incident' of the previous night, Russell broke in and said, 'Do not say a further word, my lord, for I have for ever dismissed it from my mind.' The crowded court dissolved in laughter at this bold and utterly unexpected intervention and even the offended judge joined in. But I know of no other advocate who would have dared to reprove the judge at night and then appear to forgive him next morning!

Russell was engaged in many famous cases but if I had to choose two out of the long list that seem to me the most dramatic and interesting I should choose Russell's defence of that strange and enigmatic figure – Charles Stewart Parnell – before the Parnell Commission in 1888, and the defence of Florence Maybrick at the Liverpool Assizes on 1889 on a charge of murdering her husband by the administration of arsenic.

The defence of Parnell was without doubt the most memorable experience of Russell's legal life. Lord Rosebery said of it that Russell passed at a bound from solid reputation to supreme eminence. In March of 1887 the agitation for Home Rule in Ireland was at its height. In Ireland the agitation was accompanied by scenes of great violence, and public opinion was highly inflamed. It was at this moment that *The Times* published a series of articles under the heading 'Parnellism and Crime'. The articles were designed to show that the Parnell movement was revolutionary in aim, and criminal in some of its procedure, with the ultimate purpose of destroying British government in Ireland. In April 1887 *The Times* published the famous letter, said to have been written by Parnell, condoning the dreadful murders of Lord Frederick Cavendish, the Chief Secretary for Ireland, and Mr Burke, the Under-Secretary, in Phoenix Park, Dublin. The sensation caused by the letter was immense; but Parnell contented himself by telling the House of Commons that same night that he had not written it and that it was a forgery. In view of this plain denial the matter was allowed to drop for a time; but several months later in some legal proceedings arising out of *The Times* articles, Sir Richard Webster, the Attorney General, repeated the accusation against Parnell and this compelled Parnell to take action. He asked the House of Commons to appoint a select committee to inquire whether the letter was a forgery or not. The Government set up a Special Commission composed of three judges to investigate all the charges made by *The Times*. When the Commission sat in 1888, Russell was counsel for Parnell. All the country waited for the moment when the Commission would deal with the question of the letter Parnell alleged to be a forgery. The Irish members had good reason to believe that the letter was false, and that the signature of Parnell had been forged by a man named Pigott. *The Times* had bought the letter from a Mr

Houston, the secretary of the Irish Loyal and Patriotic Union, and Houston had bought it from Pigott. The great mystery was: where had Pigott got hold of it? On 20 February 1888, Pigott went into the witness-box. He gave his evidence clearly and well: amazingly well for a man who carried such a guilty secret within his breast, as we now know that he did. He said that he had bought the letter, with other incriminating letters, in Paris from an agent who was not well disposed toward Parnell.

Now Russell was in possession of certain information about the letters that had been kept terribly secret, and for days had been pale and distraught lest this inform-ation should become known to Pigott and the Attorney General. But when Russell rose to cross-examine Pigott he regained almost in an instant his old confident bearing. His cross-examination is set out in all the books on Advocacy as a model of artistry, though in truth it was a thing of great simplicity and achieved its effect because a great master of cross-examination had carefully prepared every step. This is how it began:

'Mr Pigott, would you be good enough, with my lord's permission, to write some words on that sheet of paper for me? Perhaps you will sit down to do so.' Pigott sat down, and Russell continued: 'Now will you write the word "livelihood"?' When Pigott had done this, Russell said: 'Now just leave a space and write the word "likeli-hood".' Then after a moment, Russell said: 'Will you now write your own name?' And then: 'Will you write the word "proselytism"?' And finally: 'Will you write "Patrick Egan" and also "P. Egan"?'

Mr Barry O'Brien, who heard this cross-examination and records it fairly fully in his biography, said these last words were spoken with considerable emphasis as though they were very important.

Then Russell said in almost a careless tone: 'There is one word that I had forgotten. Lower down, please, leaving spaces, write the word "hesitancy".' And then, as though this was a vital point, he said: 'With a small "h", please.'

Now the whole point was that Pigott had used this word 'hesitancy' in one of his letters to Pat Egan, and he had spelt it 'hesitency'. Pat Egan had noticed this misspelling and he had written to Parnell to say that Pigott was the forger because he always spelt the word 'hesitancy' in this incorrect way. In another of the incriminating letters now in the possession of Russell the word hesitancy was again spelt with an 'e' where there should have been an 'a'. And on the sheet of paper which Pigott handed back to Russell in court, Pigott had spelt 'hesitancy' in the same incorrect way. These opening questions of Russell had taken about ten minutes, but when Pigott handed the paper to Russell, and Russell had read it, and saw that Pigott had spelt hesitancy with an 'e', he knew that the miserable man in the witness-box was doomed. For Russell had in his possession, all unknown to Pigott, the letters Pigott had written to Archbishop Walsh before the publication of the articles in *The Times*, showing quite plainly Pigott's knowledge of and complicity in the attempt to ruin Parnell, and by fierce and vehement questions, interspersed by damning quotations from the letters, the confident Pigott was reduced to a most pitiable spectacle, bewildered, confused, frightened, and at times saying almost anything that came into his head, however contradictory it might be.

On the first day of the cross-examination Pigott's ordeal lasted about an hour and a half. On the second day when he appeared in the witness-box he was really acknowledging defeat without actually saying so. But nobody will ever know the agony of mind through which the man passed with the knowledge that he must once more face the terrible cross-examination of Russell. On the third day when the name of Pigott was called there was no answer, but the following morning the court was informed that Pigott had written from Paris to confess the forgery. The admission itself was in a document taken down by Mr Labouchère and witnessed by George Augustus Sala. A warrant for the arrest of Pigott on a charge of perjury was issued. He was found by the police in a Madrid hotel and was allowed to go to his room to pack a few things for his journey. In a few moments there came the sound of a pistol shot. Pigott had put a bullet through his head.

This tragic ending to the central incident in the inquiry also put an end to the public interest in the remainder of the sittings of the Commission; though in a speech lasting eight days, Russell rose to great heights, and won universal praise. Russell saved Parnell in this crisis, but it was only a few years before a greater tragedy – the divorce suit – befell Parnell, and from that there was no recovery.

The other great case in which Russell was concerned was his defence of Mrs Maybrick, and it followed closely upon his triumph in the Parnell Commission. James Maybrick, a Liverpool cotton broker, died at his home under mysterious circumstances. Some of those in the house who were attending Mr Maybrick strongly suspected that Mrs Maybrick had poisoned him. She was arrested and tried for his murder at the Liverpool Assizes before Mr Justice Stephen, a great master of the English criminal law. She was convicted and sentenced to death, but the sentence was commuted to one of penal servitude for life. She served fifteen years of imprisonment and was released in 1904. The justice of her conviction was gravely questioned at the time, and the conduct of the trial and the result have been criticized ever since. Russell himself was of the opinion that Mrs Maybrick ought never to have been convicted, and he never ceased to agitate for her release, assailing Home Secretary after Home Secretary with his emphatic opinion that her continued imprisonment was a continuing injustice. In the year in which he died, he presided at the Aylesbury Assizes as Lord Chief Justice, and he went to see Mrs Maybrick in the prison there. He wrote again to the Home Secretary, telling him of Mrs Maybrick's wretchedness and imploring him to set her free. On the files at the Home Office were many reasoned letters from Russell in one of which he had said:

I have honestly tried to judge the case, and I now say that, if called upon to advise in my capacity as Head of the Criminal Courts of this country, I should advise you that Florence Maybrick ought to be allowed to go free.

And when he was made Lord Chief Justice in 1895, he wrote a letter to Mrs Maybrick saying:

I feel as strongly as I have felt from the first that you ought never to have been convicted ... and you may rest assured that I shall renew my representations for your release.

Many people have concluded that this attitude of Russell meant that he was convinced of the innocence of Mrs Maybrick but it by no means follows. When this matter was raised by Mr G. R. Sims in the pages of the newspaper *Referee*, Sir George Lewis, the famous solicitor and a personal friend of Russell, wrote to say that in all his many talks with Russell about Mrs Maybrick Russell had never once suggested that she was innocent. What he *had* said in his letters was that the case for the

Crown was not *proved*. There were, in fact, two questions to be answered in the case: Did Mr Maybrick die because of arsenical poisoning, and if he did, did Mrs Maybrick give arsenic to him with intent to murder?

Russell always maintained that Mr Maybrick died from natural causes, and the small amount of arsenic found in his body was consistent with Mr Maybrick's proved habit of taking arsenic in one form or another over some years. These questions will never be answered satisfactorily now.

There was undoubtedly a strong case against Mrs Maybrick. Mr Maybrick was aged fifty when he died and Mrs Maybrick was only twenty-six. Mr Maybrick was a healthy man, but shortly before his death he had quarrelled violently with his wife. She had cause of complaint against him concerning another woman, and Mrs Maybrick most unfortunately was carrying on an intrigue with a young man named Brierley. This intrigue was, I think, one of the reasons for her conviction on the capital charge. In late March 1889 she had spent some days with him at a London hotel as man and wife. After visiting some friends in London she returned home and with her husband went to see the Grand National at Aintree. There they met Brierley, and because of something that happened then a violent quarrel broke out when they got home, and Mr Maybrick struck his wife in the face. The family doctor managed to reconcile them, but thereafter Maybrick suddenly changed from a normally healthy man to a nervous apprehensive man, continually under the care of the doctor. In April Mrs Maybrick bought a quantity of fly-papers from several sources in Liverpool and all these fly-papers contained arsenic. She was seen by two of the servants soaking the fly-papers in water. She was seen acting suspiciously when preparing food for her husband. Mr Maybrick's last illness began in April, about a month after the fierce quarrel over Brierley. In May, Mrs Maybrick gave the nurse a letter addressed to Brierley at an address in Liverpool, and asked her to post it. Instead of doing that, Mr Maybrick's nurse opened it, because of her growing suspicions. It was a reply to Brierley, who feared that Mr Maybrick was trying to find out what happened between Mrs Maybrick and Brierley in London, and in her reply she tells Brierley he need have no fear, and adds the fatal words that were to be so prominent a feature of the trial: 'Since my return I have been nursing Maybrick night and day. *He is sick unto death* . . . and now all depends on how long his strength will last out.' The words 'sick unto death' were underlined. And three days later Mr Maybrick was dead.

The unusual feature of the trial of Mrs Maybrick was Russell's request that Mrs Maybrick should be allowed to make a statement, which the judge granted. Mrs Maybrick thereupon made a most unconvincing statement explaining the purchase of the fly-papers and the reason for doing so, and attempted to deal with some of the other serious allegations made against her. This was a mistake of the first order, and shows how the greatest of advocates are not immune from grave errors of judgement. Sir Rufus Isaacs and the Marconi shares and Sir Charles Russell in the Maybrick case are I think illustrations of such human fallibility. The law as it then stood did not permit Mrs Maybrick to go into the witness-box and give evidence on oath, but she had the right to make an unsworn statement. She made it, however, the close of the case for the defence, when corroboration of her statement by competent witnesses was not possible, and when cross-examination was out of the question. The counsel for the Crown commented on the statement in strong terms, and the learned judge said that although the defence must have known the contents of this statement for a long time, no attempt had been made in the course of the evidence for the defence to try and substantiate it; and Sir Charles Russell had paid little attention to it in his closing speech for the defence. So strong a counsel as Russell *could* have prevented Mrs Maybrick making the statement, and it must always be one of the strange features of this trial that this very great mistake was allowed to be made. When Adelaide Bartlett was defended by Edward Clarke, she said two words only, and they were 'Not guilty', and she was acquitted though the facts against her were much more deadly than they were in the case of Florence Maybrick. Edward Clarke was at liberty to make suggestions and explanations that could not be tested in any way, and he gained the verdict by sheer persuasion, unfettered by anything Adelaide Bartlett had said. Mrs Maybrick made her statement in perilous conditions, and the result was what might have been foreseen. It may very well be that it was the unsatisfactory nature of Mrs Maybrick's statement that turned the scale, for when the learned judge summed up, in an address that left much to be desired, he said these significant and rather deadly words:

'Suppose you find a man dying of arsenic, and it is proved that a person put arsenic in his plate. If he gives an explanation that you do not consider satisfactory, that is a very strong question to be considered.'

Nevertheless the verdict of guilty was received by the public with considerable astonishment and *The Times* said:

It is useless to disguise the fact that the public are not thoroughly convinced of the prisoner's guilt.

The commutation of the sentence of death relieved public opinion in some degree, but the plain fact remains that Adelaide Bartlett went free and Florence Maybrick spent the best years of her life – from twenty-six to forty-one – languishing in prison, largely I think because she wrote and underlined the words in her letter to her lover Brierley: 'He is sick unto death', and because she volunteered a statement that was not believed.

When Charles Russell died, the Bar and Bench assembled in the court of the Lord Chief Justice, and Sir Robert Finlay, the Attorney General, spoke for all when he said:

'It is, as yet, difficult to speak of Lord Russell of Killowen, particularly in this court where one still seems to see his form and his glance, and which still seems to echo his voice. In him we have lost a consummate advocate, a great judge, and a true friend. The Bar recognize that we had in him perhaps the most commanding personality that has ever adorned our great profession. By common consent no one was more desired as a colleague or more dreaded as an antagonist. His forensic eloquence recalls what was said of the greatest orator and advocate of all time: that his dominant characteristic was reason, penetrated and made red-hot by passion. He commanded success alike by the magnificent force of his personality, by the brilliance of his intellect, and by that capacity for taking pains, in which he was hardly, if ever, surpassed. Of Lord

Russell in private life and as a friend I find it difficult, if not impossible, to speak. He was simple with the simplicity of a great and kindly nature. There never was a man more thoroughly genuine. He seemed what he was and he said what he meant. He was most loved by those who knew him best, and no one who ever knew him can ever forget him.'

THOMAS ERSKINE

THOMAS ERSKINE was the very greatest advocate who ever practised at the English Bar. For myself, I cannot help regretting that he ever entered the House of Commons, or that he left the Bar to become Lord Chancellor. In Parliament he was a failure, and Romilly, the great legal reformer, voiced the general view of Erskine as Lord Chancellor, when he said: 'His incapacity for the office was too forcibly and generally felt.' But as an advocate in the courts of law, he was supreme. From 1778, when he made his first speech before the great Lord Mansfield, to the day, twenty-eight years later, when he took his seat on the Woolsack, he had no rival and no challenger. There was a time, as the eighteenth century closed, when his name was on every lip as the fearless defender of the citizen's rights; and he was hailed as the saviour of his country. Bonfires were lit in every part of the kingdom in his honour. After some of his great victories in the courts, the horses were taken out of his carriage by worshipping crowds, and he was drawn in triumph through the streets of London to his home in Serjeant's Inn. Portraits and busts of him were sold by the thousand; a hundred cities offered him their freedom; and when Lord Campbell wrote his life, he said of him:

He was the brightest ornament of which the English Bar can boast . . . and he was the charm of every society which he entered.

But two most important things must be kept in mind. Erskine's fame rests almost wholly on the magnificence of the speeches made when he was counsel for the defence in trials which excited the widest public interest. Secondly, from his very first speech in court to the last speech he made there, he was a fighter for freedom. Erskine's fame cannot therefore be separated from the circumstances of the age in which he lived or from the lasting contributions he made to it. He was continually 'breaking the rod of the oppressor'. As we look at one or two of his famous cases we shall see that he had a passion for liberty, and was able to give it noble and unforgettable expression in an age when liberty was in need of a great champion. But we shall also do well to remember the words of Lord Rosebery, when speaking of the oratory of Chatham:

The orators who impress their audience rarely impress their readers, and those who impress their readers are usually less successful with their audience. Few indeed are those that reach posterity or indeed survive a year. We cannot doubt that it is better for Chatham's fame that he was unreported . . . for his speeches would have lost half their force without the splendour of delivery.

The fame of the advocate is preserved for future ages when the causes he espoused touch the lives and liberties of men in the closest way; and the name of Erskine survives because he was fortunate enough to live in an age when the great advocate was able to make history, by defending the things which belong to the dignity and welfare of mankind. His speeches may belong to an age that is gone; but he fashioned and moulded the thoughts of men in a way that altered the very pattern of their lives, and we today enjoy their legacy. The quite astonishing thing is that this extraordinary power over the minds of men was never repeated anywhere else than in the courts of law, and Erskine's fame rests entirely upon those wonderful years of advocacy.

Erskine was born in Edinburgh in 1750. He was the youngest son of the Earl of Buchan, but was brought up in considerable poverty. He had little schooling, the most valuable part being the care with which he was taught the proper use of English. Even as a schoolboy he was ambitious to become a famous man, and earnestly wished to enter one of the learned professions. But his father and mother could not afford it, and during the years when more fortunate youths were at public schools and universities, Erskine was either a midshipman on a warship, or serving in the army. But his ambition to be famous never abated. He had married when he was twenty on the pay of an ensign in the army, and spent two years in Minorca where his regiment was stationed. Here he had leisure to devote himself to English literature and got much of Shakespeare by heart, particularly the famous speeches, as well as the works of Pope and Dryden. When the regiment returned to London, Erskine was a dashing young man of twenty-two and made a great impression in social and literary circles. He achieved a certain kind of immortality by being described by Boswell in his *Life of Johnson*. Erskine went to dinner at Sir Alexander Macdonald's and had the temerity to challenge some of Dr Johnson's opinions, and Boswell wrote of him:

. . . there was a young officer in the regimentals of the Scots Royals who talked with a vivacity, fluency, and precision so uncommon that he attracted particular attention.

But when he returned to his regiment he grew more and more dissatisfied with his position. He knew himself to be fitted for much higher things than the kind of life he was leading, and he could not bear to be condemned to obscurity and comparative poverty for the rest of his days.

I have already remarked on the element of luck or chance that enters into the life of the advocate, and a single incident at this time transformed the whole of Erskine's life. His regiment moved from one country town to another and it so happened that the Assizes were being held in one of the towns the regiment visited. Erskine, in his regimentals, quite idly entered the court where Lord Mansfield was the presiding judge. Seeing the young officer, Mansfield inquired who he was, and on hearing that he was the son of the late Earl of Buchan, whom Mansfield had known, he invited him to the Bench and explained to Erskine the nature of the case before the court. The case was being conducted by two leaders of the circuit, both quite eminent men. Erskine, with that peculiar vanity that was part of his nature, at once thought to himself that he could make a much better speech than either of the two leaders; and the thought suddenly struck him with surprising force that it was not too late to be called to the Bar himself, even though he was then twenty-four years of age. Lord Mansfield invited him to dinner and was immensely taken with his animation and the charm of his conversation. When all the guests had gone, Erskine told Mansfield that he had resolved to go to the Bar, and Mansfield did not discourage him but told him to consult his near relations. His mother very strongly approved his choice, and in the result Erskine was called to the Bar in July 1778, being then twenty-eight years of age. While he was eating his dinners at Lincoln's Inn he was living in the direst poverty, and Jeremy Bentham, who met him, said the shabbiness of his clothes was quite remarkable. But very soon all was to be changed. 'Suddenly', wrote Lord Campbell, 'he was to be the idol of all ranks of the community, and to wallow in riches. Such a quick transition from misery to splendour is only equalled in the *Arabian Nights*, when the genii of the wonderful lamp appeared, to do the bidding of Aladdin.'

If it was fate that guided the idle steps of Erskine into the assize court when the great decision to go to the Bar was made, it was surely fate that presided over the next step. It is perhaps the most important step ever made in the history of advocacy. It is certainly the most thrilling. He got his first brief when newly called to the Bar by the purest accident, and the rest he did for himself. There had been nothing like it before and there has been nothing like it since; and for once, Lord Campbell was not exaggerating when he said of Erskine's first appearance in court: 'It was the most remarkable scene ever witnessed in Westminster Hall.'

A certain Captain Baillie, in recognition of his services at sea, had been appointed Lieutenant Governor of Greenwich Hospital. He found great abuses in the administration of the hospital and made repeated requests for inquiries and redress without success. He then printed and circulated a statement setting out the facts, and criticizing Lord Sandwich, the First Lord of the Admiralty, with great and well-merited severity. Captain Baillie was immediately suspended, but although Lord Sandwich carefully kept himself in the background, he instigated others, who had likewise been criticized, to proceed against Captain Baillie for criminal libel. The trial was to come on in the Michaelmas Term, but in the long vacation fate intervened in the most remarkable way. One night a shower of rain brought

Erskine to shelter in the house of a man named Ellis, where Captain Baillie, all unknown to Erskine, was at dinner. The Greenwich Hospital case had aroused strong public feeling, and, the subject being mentioned, Erskine, fired with intense indignation, spoke with great fervour against the corrupt and tyrannical behaviour of Lord Sandwich. He left the house without being introduced to Captain Baillie, but after he had gone Baillie discovered that he had been a sailor and had been called to the Bar; and he decided there and then that Erskine should be one of his counsel. Next day the retainer was delivered at Erskine's Chambers, and a yellow golden guinea was actually put into his hand. He was vain enough to think that he was to be the only counsel for the defence, and was much mortified to learn that four other senior counsel were briefed with him. He feared he would not get a chance of saying more than a few formal words, and went to the consultation in great gloom. He found that the prosecution had offered a compromise and three of the leading counsel were in favour of accepting it, but Erskine said quite boldly: 'My advice, gentlemen, may savour more of my late profession than my present, but I am against compromising', whereupon Captain Baillie said, 'I'll be damned if I compromise', and he hugged Erskine in his excitement, exclaiming, 'You're the man for me.' When the case actually came on, the four counsel for Captain Baillie occupied the whole afternoon, and just as it was getting dark, Lord Mansfield said, believing all the counsel to have spoken, 'We will go on with this case in the morning.'

When the court met next morning it was thought that the Solicitor General would at once begin his reply, but instead of that Erskine rose from the back row and in a clear and firm voice began:

'My lord, I am likewise of counsel for the author of this supposed libel; and if the matter for consideration had been merely a question of private wrong, I should have thought myself well justified, after the very able defence made by the learned gentlemen who have spoken before me, in sparing your lordship, already fatigued with repetition, and in leaving my client to the judgement of the court. But upon an occasion of this serious and dangerous complexion – when a British subject is brought before a court of justice only for having ventured to attack abuses, which owe their continuance to the danger of attacking them – I cannot relinquish the high privilege of trying to do justice to such merit, and I will not give up even my small share of the honour of repelling and of exposing so odious a prosecution.'

The impression made upon the court by the address which followed these opening words is said to have been unprecedented, and Lord Campbell thought it to be the most wonderful forensic effort of which we have any account in our annals. The court was packed to the doors with men of the highest distinction belonging to all parties in the country. Erskine was rebuked by the greatest judge in the land for attacking Lord Sandwich when he was not before the court, but he reduced even Lord Mansfield to silence by the vehemence of his answer:

'I know that he is not *formally* before the court, but I will bring him before the court. I will drag him to light who is the dark mover behind this scene of iniquity. If Lord Sandwich keeps this man suspended, or dares to turn that suspension into a removal, I shall then not scruple to declare him an accomplice in their guilt, a shameless oppressor, a disgrace to his rank, and a traitor to his trust.'

The peroration to the speech was made in quiet and solemn tones, 'when every look was fixed upon him, where every syllable he uttered was eagerly caught up, where breathing was almost suspended, and as often as he paused, if a flake of snow had fallen, it would have been heard to fall'. That famous description always thrills me even now. In my time I have heard all the great orators in Parliament, on the platform, and in the courts of law. I have listened to almost every kind of advocate in every kind of case, but the peroration of the young Erskine still fascinates me, though the language is from another age, and would sound theatrical to modern ears. Here are the closing sentences uttered nearly two hundred years ago:

'I know that your lordships will determine according to law, and therefore if an Information should be suffered to be filed, I shall bow to the sentence and shall consider this meritorious publication to be an offence against the laws of this country; but then I shall not scruple to say that it is high time for every honest man to remove himself from a country in which he can no longer do his duty to the public with safety, where cruelty and inhumanity are suffered to impeach virtue, and where vice passes through a court of justice unpunished and unreproved.'

Captain Baillie's case was won and the victory was universally attributed to Erskine. He was overwhelmed with congratulations and when he walked through Westminster Hall he received a great ovation. When he was asked how he had the courage to stand up to Lord Mansfield he made the famous answer, 'I thought that my little children were plucking at my gown and heard them saying "Now is the time to get us bread".'

Erskine set new standards of advocacy. Until his day there were few graces of rhetoric exhibited in King's Bench courts. His strength lay in presentation. The clear statement of the facts, which is the first requirement of modern advocacy, was always observed by Erskine; and he combined with persuasive presentation of the facts a clear and compelling view of the conclusions to which he desired the court to come. At a time when the bullying of witnesses was a common practice, Erskine was always courteous and good-humoured. He united cogency and lucidity; and though his style of oratory may be unsuited to modern ears, being too ornate and too prolix, it was perfectly adapted to the age in which he lived. When the Attorney General Sir Archibald Macdonald replied to Erskine's speech in the famous case of Stockdale, charged with a libel on the House of Commons, he used these remarkable words: 'To my learned friend belong infinite eloquence and ingenuity, a gift of persuasion beyond that which I ever knew fall to any man's share, and a power of language greater than that which ever met my ear.'

And that became the universal opinion.

In 1780, only two years after his call to the Bar, he defended Lord George Gordon on a charge of high treason, the precise offence charged in the indictment being that 'he levied war against the king in his realm'. The charge was preposterous and ridiculous, but Erskine realized that if this prosecution was not defeated the liberties of individual citizens were in the direst jeopardy. Gordon was a fanatical Protestant, and at the head of 40,000 persons he led a procession to the House of Commons. There was no attack of any kind upon the constitution. Gordon and his supporters were religious-minded men and women, and their object was to present a petition for the repeal of certain modifications which had been made to mitigate the severity of the penal code as it affected Roman Catholics. Most unfortunately the procession was the forerunner of those terrible riots in London which became known as the Gordon Riots. The Government prosecuted him with immense vigour, and he was undoubtedly in the gravest danger. He had been elected the 'President of the Protestant Association' and all the dreadful sufferings of the populace were attributed to him. The members of the jury had seen their houses burnt down, the prisons broken open, fires blazing everywhere, and blood freely flowing in all parts of London. The Government confidently reckoned on a conviction to set a salutary example to others, not actuated by the same high motives as Lord George Gordon; but they reckoned without one important fact: Erskine was for the defence.

The leading counsel for the defence was Mr Kenyon, afterwards Lord Kenyon, an Equity lawyer with no talent whatever for public speaking. When he addressed the jury he apologized for being there at all by saying:

'I, who am assigned by the court to be one of his counsel, confess myself to be a person little versed in the criminal courts. I never yet stood as a counsel for a person who had so great a stake put in hazard; and therefore, gentlemen, in addressing you for him, I stand as a person in very considerable agitation of mind for the consequences which may happen through my defects.'

When he finished his speech the friends of Lord George Gordon were in an agony of apprehension for Gordon's safety. Erskine managed to get the Court to allow him to make his closing speech to the jury after all the evidence had been called for the defence. This gave him a breathing space, and it was after midnight when he rose to address the Court. The Solicitor General replied for the prosecution in the early hours of the morning and Lord Mansfield summed up at a quarter past five. The jury returned a verdict of not guilty and a notable victory for English liberties had been won. The speech of Erskine undoubtedly secured the verdict by its eloquence, its passion, and its reasoned argument. Contemporary writers speak of 'the magic of the eye, the face, the voice, and the action with which the speech was delivered', as producing an effect that was electrical, and it was the first of a series of cases in which Erskine fought with success against the efforts of the Government to misuse the processes of law for its own purposes. In this case the offence of levying war against the king in his realm was defined with complete precision by Erskine who impressed it upon the nation.

His star rose higher and higher. In 1783, after five years only at the Bar, he was given a silk gown because of his great eminence in the King's Bench, and at that time it was a very great distinction; yet it speaks volumes for the ascendancy he had gained at the Bar that the whole profession concurred in the propriety of it. Now began a series of retainers that took him to assizes in every part of the country. The first was to defend the Dean of St Asaph for publishing a seditious libel.

Now, Erskine's name is for ever associated with his victorious fights for the freedom of the Press, the independence of the Bar, and the independence of juries. His defence of the Dean of St Asaph is notable for the great fight Erskine waged to secure the right of the jury to determine whether the words complained of were a libel or not. Sir William Jones, said to be the most accomplished man of his age, had written a little tract to illustrate the main principles of government and to recommend parliamentary reform. The Dean of St Asaph, his brother-in-law, approved the tract and caused it to be reprinted and published. The government prosecuted him before Mr Justice Buller at the Shropshire Assizes. The judge ruled, contrary to Erskine's submission, that whether the words were a libel was a question of law for the judge, and the jury had nothing to do with it. This was in accordance with many decisions of Lord Mansfield as early as 1770 in certain cases arising out of the printing of the famous letters of Junius, and it was the considered view of practically all the judges. But Erskine's power over the jury was such that when they returned to court after considering their verdict, they said the Dean of St Asaph was guilty of publishing only. Then followed a most unseemly wrangle between the jury and the judge and Erskine. It illustrates the tenacity of Erskine when his convictions were roused. After considerable argument Erskine said finally: 'I insist that the word "only" shall be recorded.'

Mr Justice Buller replied: 'Then the verdict must be misunderstood; let me understand the jury.'

Erskine: 'The jury *do* understand their verdict.'

Buller: 'Sir, I will not be interrupted.'

Erskine: 'I stand here as an advocate for a brother citizen, and I desire that the word "only" shall be recorded.'

Buller: 'Sit down, Sir; remember your duty or I shall be obliged to proceed in another manner.'

Erskine: 'Your lordship may proceed in what manner you think fit; I know my duty as well as your lordship knows yours. I shall not alter my conduct.'

The jury, much upset by this altercation, finally returned their verdict as 'guilty of publishing but whether a libel or not we do not find'. On appeal, Erskine argued the point with great eloquence and learning before Lord Mansfield, Mr Justice Ashurst, and Mr Justice Willes. Mansfield and Ashurst supported Mr Justice Buller, but Mr Justice Willes dissented on one important point. He said that a jury could give a general verdict of acquittal without being obliged to give their reasons. This dissenting judgment was given statutory effect in Fox's Libel Act of 1792, but before that triumphant day came, Erskine fought and won a series of cases that established the rights of juries beyond all question, and it was the result of these cases that made Erskine a popular hero.

In 1789 came the great case of John Stockdale in which Erskine is said to have made the finest speech ever delivered in any court in England, and Lord Campbell said that the verdict he gained established for ever the freedom of the press in England. Pending the impeachment of Warren Hastings, after the articles against him, drawn in very provocative language by no less a person than Edmund Burke, had been published in every newspaper in the land, together with some inflammatory speeches made in the House of Lords, a Minister of the Church of Scotland, a Mr Logan, wrote a pamphlet in defence of Hastings which criticized the prosecution with great vigour. The House of Commons, it was said, in making one of the charges, was compared to 'a tribunal of inquisition' rather than a court of Parliament. Mr Stockdale, a bookseller in London, published the pamphlet in the ordinary way of his business. It had a very great sale, and on the motion of Charles James Fox the House of Commons prayed that

Mr Stockdale be proceeded against for a libel upon the House of Commons. Again it was a preposterous prosecution, and the *Edinburgh Review* said of Erskine's defence of Stockdale and freedom of speech that: 'It is justly regarded by all English lawyers as a consummate specimen of the art of addressing a jury – as a standard, a sort of precedent for treating cases of libel'. Some passages of the speech can well be recalled today with a recognition of their immense value at the critical time when the words were spoken. For instance these words which occur towards the end of Erskine's address:

'From minds thus subdued by the terrors of punishment, there could issue no works of genius to expand the empire of human reason, nor any masterly compositions on the general nature of government, by the help of which the great commonwealths of mankind have founded their establishments. . . . Under such terrors all the great lights of science and civilization must be extinguished; for men cannot communicate their free thought to one another with a lash held over their heads.'

The jury found a verdict of not guilty, and a very great triumph for the right of free expression of opinion had been won.

Many other cases made Erskine's name memorable, including the famous defence of Tom Paine when Paine was charged with publishing a seditious libel contained in *The Rights of Man*. But I want to take leave of Erskine with an account of the greatest victory of all.

At the close of the eighteenth century many societies had been formed for the purpose of advancing the cause of parliamentary reform. The government of the day most misguidedly decided to prosecute the members of these societies, by resorting to the law of 'constructive treason' which had received such a blow on the trial of Lord George Gordon. If these prosecutions had succeeded, all political agitation in England would have been banned, at least for a very long time, because the advocates of reform were actually charged with seeking to bring about a revolution in this country, and so constructively 'to compass the death of our Lord the King'. In his defence of Hardy, Horne-Tooke, and Thelwall on these charges, for which he took no fee, Erskine not only secured their acquittal, but compelled the Government to abandon all the other outstanding prosecutions against all other defendants; and thus preserved for that generation the right, so justly cherished in our own, to agitate by all lawful means for the causes in which men and women believe.

Erskine had the imperfections of which I have written, but in the eloquence with which he expounded great causes and advocated great principles in the courts of law, he excelled all who had gone before him, and all who have since followed him; and by so doing he has given to the long and illustrious roll of human benefactors his own imperishable name.

THE ART OF ADVOCACY

I SHOULD like to conclude these sketches of great advocates by saying something about the place of the advocate in our society, and the problems and the pleasures that belong to the advocate's vocation. I fully realize that when men speak of advocacy they usually refer to advocacy in the courts of law, and almost always to the moments of high drama in great criminal trials. But I want to treat advocacy in rather a wider sense because I believe that advocacy is very much more than a mere legal accomplishment. Advocacy in the courts must always take pride of place because the opportunities for its most effective use are chiefly to be found there; but I like to think that every day the art of advocacy is being employed in much wider fields – in Parliament, in the churches, on the platform – and indeed everywhere that men and women meet to listen to one of their fellows expounding some subject or theme in order to win the allegiance of the particular audience. I shall therefore speak of what I think is the most important element in all advocacy, whether in the courts of law or elsewhere, and that is the art of attractive and persuasive speech on all occasions that call for its exercise.

But before I do that there is one important matter concerning the advocate and his work with which I ought to deal briefly. Many, I know, regard the law as something of a mystery, and I am quite conscious of the prejudice against the advocate which exists in the minds of many members of the public. I cannot hope to remove that prejudice, but I am sure that I ought to try to do so. From the moment that I was called to the Bar I have been brought face to face with the widespread misconception of the true function of the advocate in our courts of law and of his place in our way of life. There cannot be any member of the Bar who has not been faced at some time or other with the old and familiar question: 'How can you possibly defend a guilty man?' or some question of a similar kind. Such questions were asked at Athens in the days of Demosthenes and at Rome in the days of Cicero and they have been asked at every stage of our own legal history. These questions have been answered by great judges, such as Mr Justice Crampton in the famous case of the Queen versus O'Connell, by great advocates such as Erskine in the trial of Tom Paine, and by great men such as Dr Johnson – but the prejudice still persists, and the questions are still asked. I quite realize how strange and indeed wrong it must seem to the ordinary citizen, that a man of honour and integrity and usually of great gifts should defend a man that he must know in his heart to be guilty of the crime with which he is charged and to be paid for doing so. 'How is it possible', men say, 'for an advocate to resist an argument that appears to be founded on truth, and to seek to make the worse appear the better reason?' For, put quite starkly, the charge against the advocate is: that he cannot possibly be sincere or indeed honest in the conduct of his profession; for the ordinary citizen only espouses some particular cause because he believes in it, but the advocate espouses a cause because he is paid to do so, whether he believes in it or not. I do not think it is a sufficient answer to say that theoretically, at least, the advocate has no choice in the kind of case he will take up. In practice, if there are good reasons why an advocate should not undertake a certain case, he can quite easily decline it. But, as Erskine so eloquently said, 'If the advocate refuses to defend from what he may think of the charge or the defence, he assumes the character of the judge . . . and puts the heavy influence of perhaps a mistaken opinion into the scale against the accused, in whose favour the benevolent principles of English Law makes all presumptions, and which commands the very judge to be his counsel.'

Still, the charge against the advocate remains and was put into its most deadly form by that strange and erratic genius, Dean Swift, in *Gulliver's Travels*, when he said of the Bar that 'they were a society of men bred up from their youth in the art of proving by words multiplied for the purpose, that white is black and black is white according as they are paid.' Now the plain truth is that when the advocate is pleading in any case, *he is not stating his own view*, and indeed has no right whatever to do so. He is bound by very strict rules of conduct and an equally strict code of honour, expressly designed to allow him to discharge his duty in the administration of justice without being false to himself or to his conscience and without failing in his duty to the community in which he lives. The function of the advocate is to present one side of the case with all the skill he possesses, so that the judge, or the judge and jury, can compare *his* presentation with that of the counsel on the other side and then decide after full investigation, where the truth lies. In a criminal case many people suppose that an advocate who is prosecuting in a case of murder is trying to get the accused convicted at all costs. I speak with knowledge when I say that the duty of prosecuting counsel is to act as a minister of justice in the fullest sense. He must make sure that the evidence is relevant and admissible and is presented without bias. He must also make sure that the evidence in favour of the prisoner is before the court, and is given the same prominence and emphasis as the evidence tendered to show his guilt. And he will never omit to tell the jury that the duty of the prosecution is to prove the case against the accused beyond all reasonable doubt.

And what is the duty of the advocate who shoulders the heavy burden of *defending* the prisoner on this gravest of all charges? It is to devote himself completely to his task whatever he himself may think of the charges, and to lay aside every other duty, so that he may watch constantly in the interests of the accused, and say for him all that he would wish to say for himself, were he able to do so. The purpose of this procedure in English law is not that a guilty person shall escape, but to make certain, so far as human fallibility can do so, that no innocent person shall suffer. I sometimes hear it said that verdicts of not guilty are obtained from juries against the weight of the evidence by brilliant advocacy, such as Edward Clarke displayed in the defence of Adelaide Bartlett; and it may very well be so. But while human nature remains what it is, juries will *acquit* against the weight of the evidence, but they will not *convict* against the weight of the evidence, whatever the nature of the advocacy for the prosecution. I hope I have made it plain how wise is the rule which forbids the advocate to express his own view on the case in which he is engaged. Let me illustrate its wisdom.

In the famous case of William Palmer, the Rugeley poisoner, charged with murder, his counsel was Mr Serjeant Shee, afterwards Mr Justice Shee. In addressing the jury the learned Serjeant said:

'I begin Palmer's defence and say in all sincerity that I have an entire conviction of his innocence.'

The case was being tried at the Old Bailey before three judges, and I have always been surprised that Lord Chief Justice Campbell, who presided, did not intervene at once to rebuke so outrageous a departure from the long tradition. But Sir Alexander Cockburn, the Attorney General, who prosecuted, said to the jury when he addressed them:

'Gentlemen, you have heard from my learned friend the unusual and, I think I may say, the unprecedented assurance of his conviction of his client's innocence. I can only say that I think it would have been better if my learned friend had abstained from so strange a declaration. What would he think of me, if, imitating his example, I at this moment stated to you on my honour, as he did, what is my conviction from a conscientious consideration of this case. The best rebuke which I can administer is to abstain from imitating so dangerous an example'.

And when Lord Campbell summed-up to the jury, he said on this matter:

'I most strongly recommend to you that you should attend to everything Serjeant Shee said to you with the exception of his own private opinion. It is my duty to tell you that opinion ought not to be any ingredient in your verdict. It would be disastrous if a jury was led to believe that a prisoner is not guilty because his advocate expresses his perfect conviction of his innocence. And on the other hand, if an advocate withholds his opinion, the jury may suppose that he is conscious of his client's guilt; whereas it is the duty of the advocate to press his *argument* upon the jury, but not his *opinion*.'

Palmer was convicted and hanged, but there is very

good reason for thinking that he had committed other murders beside the one for which he was hanged; and how Serjeant Shee could have expressed his belief in Palmer's innocence with any sense of conviction is almost beyond belief. It must be admitted that there are times when the advocate is placed in great difficulty, when the plea to be made in the case conflicts violently either with his own knowledge or his own judgment of the situation. The case most often quoted is that of a brilliant Irishman named Charles Phillips, who had been called to the English Bar. In 1840 he was briefed to defend a Swiss man-servant named Courvoisier on a charge of murder. Courvoisier was the personal servant of Lord William Russell and one morning Lord Russell was found horribly murdered in his bed. The motive of the murder was robbery, and, after investigation, the police arrested the man-servant and charged him with the murder. In the middle of the trial at the Old Bailey when Phillips was conducting a brilliant defence, the prisoner asked to speak with him, and he then told Phillips that he had committed the murder, and added these most surprising words: 'And now I rely on you to do the best you can to prove that I have not.' So distressed was Phillips that he consulted Baron Parke, who was taking no part in the case, but happened to be sitting by the side of the Lord Chief Justice who was presiding over the trial. When Baron Parke heard that the prisoner insisted on Phillips continuing to defend him, Parke told Phillips that his duty was to continue, and to use all fair arguments arising out of the evidence. Most people seem to agree that this was proper advice, though some doubt it; but Phillips was obviously put into the greatest difficulty. His subsequent conduct brought the most violent criticism on his head, for it was said (quite falsely, I think) that he had suggested that the crime was committed by some other person. The words in which he is supposed to have done this have been preserved and they read like this:

'But you will say to me, if the prisoner did not do it, who did do it? Ask not me, a poor finite creature like yourselves. Ask the prosecutor who did it. It is for him to tell you who did it; and until he shall have proved by the clearest evidence that it was the prisoner at the Bar, beware how you imbrue your hands in the blood of that young man.'

It is a very nice question whether in speaking these words, and others like them, Phillips was acting wrongly; but the widespread public controversy which followed the execution of Courvoisier showed the intense public interest in what are the duties of the advocate in the courts of law, and the manner in which he discharges them. Everybody was agreed that Phillips was not entitled to suggest that some other person had committed the crime, and that most emphatically he had no right whatever to declare his own conviction about the guilt of the accused. I have mentioned this case because many people believe that this kind of situation frequently arises. I am quite sure it does not. In my experience it is exceedingly rare. On the occasions when a prisoner pleads guilty, the advocate is entitled to plead in mitigation of sentence, and bring to the attention of the Court any circumstances that might affect the question of punishment or treatment.

Let me now end this brief discussion of the ethics of advocacy with a few wise sentences from the great Dr Johnson. Boswell records Johnson as saying:

We talked of the practice of the law. Sir William Forbes said he thought an honest lawyer should never undertake a cause which he was satisfied was not a just one. 'Sir,' said Dr Johnson, 'a lawyer has no business with the justice or injustice of the cause which he undertakes, unless the client asks his opinion, and then he is bound to give it honestly. The justice or injustice of the cause is to be decided by the judge. Consider, Sir, what is the purpose of courts of justice? It is that every man shall have his case fairly tried by men appointed to try causes. . . . A lawyer is not to usurp the province of the jury or the judge and determine what shall be the effect of the evidence or the result of legal argument. . . . If lawyers were to undertake no such causes until they were sure that they were just, a man might be precluded altogether from a trial of his claim, though were it judicially examined it might be found a very *just* claim.'

I now turn to that element in advocacy which I have described as the proper use of attractive and persuasive speech. It is not confined to the advocate in the courts of law; it is within the reach of all who aspire to influence their fellows in any walk of life, but the price to be paid is one of taking pains and exercising much patience. Most people find pleasure in hearing their own language spoken with ease and grace, and a surprising number of people cherish a secret ambition to speak it gracefully themselves, both in ordinary conversation and in more formal and pre-meditated speech. This is much to be commended, for we have inherited a language 'malleable and pliant as Attic, dignified as Latin, dulcet as Italian, sonorous as Spanish', as Quiller-Couch described it; and we have as part of our heritage a long and splendid tradition of great oratory. I can never read the famous tribute of Ben Jonson to the speaking of Francis Bacon without wishing that I could have heard him, for I confess to a love of the spoken word as some men love great music, and a select few love great poetry. For this is what Ben Jonson said:

His hearers could not cough or look aside from him without loss. . . . No man had their affections more in his power. The fear of every man that heard him was lest he should make an end.

Significantly enough, the reputation of some of our greatest orators rests on the reports of those that *heard* them and whose reports have been preserved. The immense fame of Lord Chatham lives on to this day, but the spell of the orator is preserved for us by people who heard him speak, as Horace Walpole did. When Sheridan made his great speech at the trial of Warren Hastings, Charles James Fox, Edmund Burke, and the younger Pitt, all of them great masters of English speech, acclaimed the speech of Sheridan as something quite phenomenal, Pitt actually saying that, 'It surpassed all the eloquence of ancient and modern times.' The speech can be read today, but nobody can hope to recapture the wonder and the glory of the spoken word which called forth the rapturous language of some of the very greatest orators of their time. And yet the wonder and the glory must have been there. It is precisely this same element in great advocacy that is beyond analysis. When James Russell Lowell recalled the eloquence of the spoken word of Emerson, he said:

> 'Was never eye did see that face,
> Was never ear did hear that tongue,
> Was never mind did mind his grace
> That ever thought the travail long;
> But eyes and ears and every thought
> Were with his sweet perfections caught.'

It was the distinctive quality of personality that gave the compelling power to Emerson's speaking, and all the great advocates I have known and all the great orators I have heard had this great and indispensable quality. It must be frankly admitted that the speeches of great advocates at their highest and best are not quite in the same class as the truly great orators such as Sir Winston Churchill was in 1940, with the possible exception of Erskine. But the same considerations apply to both oratory in general and to forensic oratory in particular, and also to the more modest speaking of the general run of mankind. The effect achieved depends on the character and quality of the speaker himself, the occasion on which he speaks, the subject-matter of the speech, and the form in which the speech is cast. It is sometimes said that the whole art of advocacy consists in presentation. The late Lord Simon had many shining gifts, but everybody agrees that his strength lay in his wonderful power of presentation. Sometimes he had to present to the court cases of great complexity and of great magnitude. I have frequently heard him transform what might have been, in other hands, a dry and fatiguing recitation of facts into an enthralling narrative told with matchless skill, in language of the simplest and most lucid kind. Voice, gesture, knowledge, language, emotion – all go into the art of presentation; but it is not too much to say that all these things will fall short of their full effect if the presentation of the case is not above all other things *orderly*. Mr Justice Maule is affectionately remembered by generations of lawyers for the wisdom that lay concealed behind his rich humour. One of his most famous observations was on this very matter of presentation. Provoked by the confused, blundering way in which an advocate was presenting a bewildering array of facts to the jury, Mr Justice Maule said:

'Mr Smith, do you not think by introducing a little order into your narrative you might possibly render yourself a trifle more intelligible? It may be my fault that I cannot follow you – I know that my brain is getting a little dilapidated; but I should like to stipulate for some sort of order. There are plenty of them. There is the chronological, the botanical, the metaphysical, the geographical, why even the alphabetical order would be better than no order at all.'

Advocacy in the courts of law has a special technique of its own which is only of interest to those who practise it. Nothing can equal the experience of seeing the great advocates at work in the courts and catching the magic of the spoken word, for it is not so much what is said but the manner in which it is said that matters. For example, the advocate in the criminal court follows quite a distinct career from that of the advocate who confines himself to the Chancery Division. I well remember one of the earliest cases in which I was concerned after coming to London. Up to then I had been concerned with what is sometimes called 'the rough and tumble of the common law', which meant county courts and magistrate's courts in and around Birmingham, with occasional visits to quarter sessions and assizes. I suddenly found myself as a junior counsel, surrounded by the most distinguished silks of the Chancery Division, defending in some misfeasance summonses brought by the Liquidator of one of the companies of Ernest Terah Hooley. Frankly, I didn't think the Chancery Leaders were as good at cross-examination as some of the counsel in Birmingham, but when the Chancery Leaders addressed the judge on the law, I was almost lost, as it were, in 'wonder, love, and praise'. I had never heard anything quite like it before, but I had, at least, the sense to know that it was advocacy of the very highest kind, and of a very rare and special kind at that. When in later years I was led in the Court of Appeal by Sir John Simon, and by the present Lord Simonds, then Mr Gavin Simonds, in the House of Lords in the Portuguese Bank Note case, I heard again the self-same quality of advocacy and felt the same sense of exaltation.

But if the all-important task of the great advocate is to persuade, whether it be in the Chancery Division or the courts of common law, there are certain things which the ordinary run of advocates do well to observe. Whatever the case and whatever the court, the first and vital thing is that the advocate shall know the case he desires to make with complete thoroughness. He must have a complete mastery of the facts and he must have the power to present them in the most attractive way. He must have a quick mind and an understanding heart. He must acquire in some way an insight into human nature and a natural unforced sympathy with all sorts and conditions of men. Above all, he must have what I can only call an intuitive recognition of what the circumstances of the case require as it slowly unfolds itself before the court.

The other most important part of the advocate's equipment is command of language. It enriches and adorns almost every other quality. Lord Macmillan once said that no advocate can be a great pleader who has not a sense of literary form and whose mind is not stored with the treasures of our great literary inheritance upon which he may draw at will. I am not sure that this is not putting the case a little too high, but there can be no doubt about the power which comes from a thorough acquaintance with the language and the use of what Swift called 'proper words in proper places'. When Sir Winston Churchill was surveying 'the dark wide field' of the first year of the war to the House of Commons in 1940, he suddenly broke off a detailed account of the country's defences and spoke the famous sentence about 'so much being owed by so many to so few'. That was a perfect illustration of the power which comes from the sense of literary form, for his words, so exquisite in their form, and so beautiful in their simplicity, voiced the feelings of millions of hearts so that the words have not merely gone into our common speech but, like the reputed saying of Pericles 'of famous men the whole earth is the tomb', they will be quoted so long as the language lasts as one of the great sayings of the world.

The advocate, then, must be a student of words; he must know something of their history, their sound, their meaning, their associations, and above all the use that has been made of them by the great masters of the tongue. It is well if he knows the Bible in the Authorized Version, and if he has made the language of the book of Common Prayer his very own. It is well, too, if he knows something of the great triumvirate Chaucer, Shakespeare, and Dryden, who did so much to mould and fashion the language we speak, and of writers like Swift, Sterne, and Defoe and the other great stylists. For I am one of those who believe that in the ordinary everyday affairs of life, even in casual conversation, the use of graceful and simple English is an accomplishment greatly to be desired. And how much more is it to be desired when the whole purpose of the advocate in the courts or outside the courts is to gain the ends he seeks by the impression he creates upon the particular tribunal before which he appears.

Many opinions have been expressed from time to time about the character of the highest advocacy and the highest oratory. It would seem to be the view of those best qualified to judge that simplicity of speech, linked with the expression of the deepest feelings of mankind, has always had power to stir men's blood in all ages of the world's history, and the great names of Abraham Lincoln and John Bright are used as perennial examples.

Perhaps I might be allowed to end on a personal note. For more than forty years I have been actively engaged in the practice of the law, either as counsel or as judge, and during that time I have seen, I suppose, almost every kind of case, in almost every kind of court, and almost every kind of advocate and judge. I am quite sure that when men and women are brought into the civil or criminal courts, for whatever reason, they should be able to turn for assistance at what may be the critical moments of their lives to a trained body of advocates, independent and fearless, who are pledged to see that they are protected against injustice and that their rights are not wrongly invaded from any quarter. The vocation of the advocate calls for the nicest sense of honour and for a complete devotion to the ideals of justice, and I believe it to be a lofty and necessary calling which is vital for the maintenance of that way of life in which we have come to believe. To that great calling men and women might well devote their greatest gifts and their highest powers, as did the six great advocates whose fame it has been my privilege to recall.